The Eighteenth and Twenty-First Amendments

Other titles in *The Constitution:*

The First Amendment
Freedom of Speech, Religion, and the Press
ISBN: 0-89490-897-9

The Second Amendment
The Right to Own Guns
ISBN:0-89490-925-8

The Fourth Amendment
Search and Seizure
ISBN: 0-89490-924-X

The Fifth Amendment
The Right to Remain Silent
ISBN: 0-89490-894-4

The Thirteenth Amendment
Ending Slavery
ISBN: 0-89490-923-1

The Fifteenth Amendment
African-American Men's Right to Vote
ISBN: 0-7660-1033-3

The Eighteenth and Twenty-First Amendments
Alcohol—Prohibition and Repeal
ISBN: 0-89490-926-6

The Nineteenth Amendment
Women's Right to Vote
ISBN: 0-89490-922-3

The Eighteenth and Twenty-First Amendments

Alcohol—Prohibition and Repeal

The
Constitution

Eileen Lucas

Enslow Publishers, Inc.

40 Industrial Road   PO Box 38
Box 398   Aldershot
Berkeley Heights, NJ 07922   Hants GU12 6BP
USA   UK

http://www.enslow.com

Library of Congress Cataloging-in-Publication Data

Lucas, Eileen.
    The Eighteenth and Twenty-First Amendments :
alcohol—prohibition and repeal / Eileen Lucas.
       p. cm. — (The Constitution)
    Summary: Discusses the political and social aspects of
the Eighteenth Amendment prohibiting the sale and
consumption of alcoholic beverages, as well as the repeal of
that law with the passage of the Twenty-First Amendment.
    ISBN 0-89490-926-6
    1. United States. Constitution. 18th Amendment—
Juvenile literature—History. 2. United States. Constitution.
21st Amendment—Juvenile literature—History.
3. Prohibition—United States—Juvenile literature—
History. 4. Constitutional amendments—United States
Juvenile literature—History. [1. United States.
Constitution. 2. Prohibition.] I. Title. II. Series:
Constitution (Springfield, Union County, N.J.)
KF3919.L83   1998
344.73'0541—DC21   97-20073
                                      CIP
                                        AC

Photo Credits: Bentley Historical Library, University of Michigan, pp.
39, 51, 55, 79; Library of Congress, pp. 9, 29, 33, 36, 42, 57, 72, 75;
National Archives, pp. 13, 22, 27, 47, 65, 69, 81, 84, 93.

Cover Photo: Bettmann

Contents

The Death of John Barleycorn

In Norfolk, Virginia, the church bells began ringing at one minute past midnight on January 17, 1920. The bells tolled for the death of John Barleycorn, an imaginary man who symbolized the evils of alcohol.

Ten thousand prohibitionists, people in favor of prohibiting, or outlawing, the sale of alcohol, gathered for a mock funeral. The service was led by the Reverend Billy Sunday. He was a baseball-player-turned-preacher who had once said, "I hope in the wise providence of God that I may be permitted to preach the funeral service over the liquor traffic."[1] With the Eighteenth Amendment that went into effect as the bells tolled, forbidding the manufacture, sale, importation, exportation, or transportation of intoxicating liquors in the United States, it appeared that his wish had come true.

As he stood before a twenty-foot casket, Reverend Sunday's voice boomed out these words: "Good-bye John. You were God's worst enemy. You were Hell's best friend."[2] A man dressed in a devil's costume danced around while other actors pretended to mourn for Barleycorn.

Reverend Sunday continued:

> The reign of tears is over. The slums will soon be only a memory. We will turn our prisons into factories and our jails into storehouses and corncribs. Men will walk upright now, women will smile, and children will laugh. Hell will be forever for rent.[3]

The casket was paraded through the streets of Norfolk on a horse-drawn hearse.

This ceremony in Norfolk was one of the biggest, but certainly not the only, celebration as the Eighteenth Amendment took effect. Churches and towns across America rang their bells and lit their lights. There were parades and meetings and prayer services. ". . . [L]et there be great rejoicing, for an enemy the equal of Prussianism [the Germans just defeated in the First World War] . . . has been overthrown and victory crowns the efforts of the forces of righteousnes [sic] . . .," said the invitations to a celebration given by the local Women's Christian Temperance Union.[4]

"Now for an era of clear thinking and clean living!" cheered a press release for the Anti-Saloon League.[5] Sure, there might be *some* problems trying to enforce the law, but most Americans were law-abiding and most states already had some laws restricting alcohol use in some form anyway.

Enough Americans had come to support prohibition to make the Eighteenth Amendment's passage through Congress and the state lawmaking bodies relatively swift and easy. It seemed only a matter of time before America would be a nation completely free of alcohol. Wayne Wheeler of the Anti-Saloon League predicted that, after a year of

With the passage of the Eighteenth Amendment, prohibitionists celebrated the apparent end of alcohol's presence in the lives of Americans. This mock tombstone was erected to mark the "death" of John Barleycorn, an imaginary man who symbolized all that was evil about alcohol.

strict enforcement, federal funds for upholding the law could probably be cut. John F. Kramer, the first Prohibition Commissioner, stated: "this law will be obeyed in cities large and small."[6]

As the funeral for John Barleycorn was being held in Norfolk, federal prohibition agents prepared to enforce the law. They entered a restaurant in New York and smashed the whiskey bottles they found there. A supply of wine bottles found near the Iron River in Michigan was also destroyed.

But even as these law enforcers were trying to show that the law meant what it said, members of the criminal world were preparing to get around it. Within an hour of the official start of prohibition, six masked men broke into a railroad yard in Chicago and stole one hundred thousand dollars' worth of liquor that was marked for medical use.

For the next thirteen years, the subject of alcohol would be a national obsession in the United States. The pros and cons of life under the Eighteenth Amendment were hotly debated by drys, who supported it, and wets, who opposed it. The wets finally won, and the Eighteenth Amendment was repealed, or overturned, with the Twenty-First Amendment, in 1933.

To this day, the Eighteenth Amendment remains the only amendment to the United States Constitution ever to be repealed. This book will examine the fascinating story of how the American government came to try what would be called "a noble experiment," and what happened when the people decided that it had failed. It is the story of preachers and gangsters, politicians and teachers, men, women, and children. To begin, we will look at its place in the United States Constitution.

The Constitution and Its Amendments

On May 25, 1787, twenty-nine representatives of various states gathered at the Pennsylvania State House. Most of them knew each other, and this setting, very well. Many of them had been members of the Continental Congress, a group that had gathered here in 1775 to discuss the issues of British rule over the colonies. The representatives had also gathered here when the Declaration of Independence was signed in 1776.

But now, having fought the Revolutionary War (1775–1783), which led to the birth of a new nation—the United States—and established the Articles of Confederation to govern the newly created states, they were gathered once again. The Articles of Confederation were proving inadequate to govern the new country. They had come together to correct the situation, to amend the articles.

On the third day, however, Edmund Randolph of Virginia made a proposal that would mean that, instead of amending the Articles of Confederation, the representatives would in fact be creating a whole new kind of national government. Over a period of several months, they crafted a constitution. They hoped it would be strong enough to hold the nation together, but not so strong as to threaten the people's rights. The representatives debated the needs of large states and small, the northerly and the southernmost, and repeatedly compromised to reach agreement. On September 17, 1787, the delegates signed the Constitution of the United States. In light of the topic of this book, it is interesting to note that, according to the diary of George Washington, having completed their business, "the members adjourned to the City Tavern, dined together and took a cordial leave of each other."[1]

The delegates recognized that the Constitution they wrote was not perfect. The Founding Fathers (those who helped to establish the United States government) knew that there would be a need for changes from time to time. "The warmest friends and the best supporters the Constitution has do not contend that it is free from imperfection," wrote George Washington to his nephew in 1787.[2] Washington and the other Founding Fathers wanted the American people to be able to change the Constitution when necessary. On the other hand, they did not want it to be so easy to change that it would be amended too quickly, frequently, or carelessly. They included procedures for how it could be amended so that these problems could be avoided.

Article V of the Constitution deals with amendments. It states that either house of Congress can propose amendments, or the lawmakers of two thirds of the states can call for a convention to propose an amendment. The second option has never been

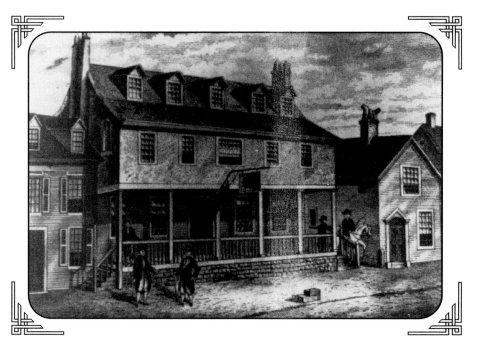

*After finishing the business of writing the Constitution, the
Founding Fathers enjoyed an evening of celebration at the
City Tavern before going their separate ways.*

exercised. So far, all amendments to the Constitution have been proposed by Congress. The proposed amendment must then be ratified, or agreed to, by three fourths of the states, either by their state lawmakers, or by conventions called for that purpose in each of the states. The Twenty-First Amendment, which repealed the Eighteenth, would be the first to call for the convention procedure to ratify an amendment.

Once an amendment is ratified, Congress has to pass laws to regulate and enforce the amendment. It is up to the President to ensure that the amendment and the laws are enforced. The Supreme Court determines whether the enforcing laws are constitutional. In order for an amendment, or the Constitution as a whole, to be effective, the people have to know that the government stands behind it.

No sooner was the Constitution ratified and George Washington elected President, than work began on the first amendments. Several of the states had accepted the Constitution only with the understanding that the Bill of Rights would be added.

On December 15, 1791, with the approval of three fourths of the states (eleven out of fourteen), ten amendments were added to the Constitution. Together these ten amendments are known as the Bill of Rights. They guarantee such rights as freedom of speech, freedom of religion, and the right to "due process," or fairness, in courts of law. The Eleventh Amendment was added three years later. It prevented a resident of one state from suing another state.

In 1803, Congress proposed the Twelfth Amendment to change the way the President and Vice President of the United States were elected. Originally, members of the electoral college each got two votes.

(The electoral college is a group of representatives chosen by the voters of each state to elect the President and Vice President of the United States.) The person with the most votes became President and the runner-up became Vice President. This presented a problem in 1800 when there was a tie between Thomas Jefferson and Aaron Burr. With the Twelfth Amendment, ratified in 1804, the electoral college would vote separately for President and Vice President.

After that, there were no more amendments ratified for over fifty years. Not until the Civil War (1861–1865) were any further amendments passed. The Thirteenth Amendment formally and forever abolished (ended) slavery in the United States. It was proposed by Congress on January 31, 1865, a few months before the Civil War came to an end. It was ratified on December 18, 1865. Previous amendments had mostly dealt with the way things were done by the federal government. This amendment was different, however. It created a restriction on something that had previously been considered a concern of individual states.

The Fourteenth Amendment was written to make sure that newly freed slaves could not be denied citizenship and to declare that states could not deny the rights of citizens. The Fifteenth Amendment declared that citizens could not be denied the right to vote on the basis of race. Both the Fourteenth and Fifteenth Amendments were largely ignored and unenforced for many years in much of the United States.

The Sixteenth Amendment gave Congress the right to collect income taxes. It resulted in the wealthy paying more tax than the poor, and became part of the Constitution on February 5, 1913. The Seventeenth allowed the people to vote for senators rather than having them chosen by state lawmakers. It was ratified only two months after the Sixteenth Amendment in May 1913. Both of these amendments were the result of reform-minded movements. Social reform activists would also play an important role in the fight for the Eighteenth Amendment.

As will be seen in following chapters, the movement to reform the American people by means of a constitutional amendment prohibiting the use of alcohol had been growing for many years. The movement was especially strong in the years following the Civil War. A number of states, mostly in the South and Midwest, passed laws creating varying degrees of "dryness," or prohibition of alcohol.

It was another war, World War I (1914–1918), that gave the final push to prohibition. First there was the need to conserve grain for bread instead of distilling it into alcohol. Another factor was the wartime prejudice against Germans and anything German. This included beer and the brewing industry.

On August 1, 1917, the Senate voted sixty-five to twenty in favor of a constitutional amendment to prohibit the manufacture and sale of alcohol in the United States. On December 18, 1917, the Eighteenth Amendment proposal was also accepted by the House of Representatives by a vote of 282 to 128. It was then sent to the states for ratification. Mississippi was the first to ratify, on January 8, 1918. On January 16, 1919, just over a year later, Nebraska became the thirty-sixth state to ratify. The Eighteenth Amendment then became part of the Constitution. As the amendment stated, it would take effect one year from that date.

In 1920 and 1933, the Nineteenth and Twentieth Amendments were passed. The Nineteenth gave women the right to vote. The Twentieth advanced the President's inauguration from March 4 to January 20. Also, senators and congressmen elected in November would take office January 3, instead of waiting until the following December. This shortened the "lame duck" period, the time between an election and the date when new candidates actually take office.

Then, in 1933, an amendment to repeal the Eighteenth Amendment was passed in both the House and the Senate and was sent to the states. It was quickly ratified, and became the Twenty-First Amendment on December 5, 1933. National prohibition, also known as the "noble experiment," was over.

In the years since 1933, six more amendments have been added to the Constitution, bringing the total to twenty-seven. Some ten thousand amendments have been suggested in Congress during the two hundred plus years since the Constitution was signed. Only thirty-four have received Congressional approval and been sent to the states for ratification. Just twenty-seven of the thirty-four have actually made it into the Constitution.

It would seem that the goals of the Founding Fathers have been met. It *is* possible to amend the Constitution, but it does not happen very easily or very frequently. When an amendment is needed, it can become part of the Constitution. When an amendment is seen as having failed, as was the case with the Eighteenth, it can be repealed. That is how the Constitution continues to serve the needs of the American people and their government so long after the Founding Fathers adjourned to the City Tavern.

Rum and Reform

There was little room for anything but the necessities of life on board the ships that brought the first Europeans to North America in the 1600s. Among those things considered necessities were barrels of alcohol. When supplies brought from Europe ran out, colonists turned to making their own.

Colonial Customs

Alcoholic drinks were a popular beverage. Drinking water could not always be trusted as safe, and at times was unavailable. Without refrigeration, milk spoiled quickly. Coffee and tea had to be imported. Wine, beer, rum, whiskey, and hard cider could be produced locally. Besides, moderate amounts of alcohol were considered a safeguard against many kinds of illnesses, and a cure for others. Even children were given alcohol occasionally. Perhaps this was done in the hope that small amounts now would prevent excessive use later.

Colonists drank at all different times of day, and at

most gatherings. Some even drank at church. A Quaker informed others gathered at a prayer meeting in the early 1770s that he was "oppress'd [sic] with the smell of rum from the breaths of those who sat around him."[1] Records show that the American of Colonial days drank at seed time, at harvest time, and in between. He drank to pass the time of day with a neighbor—or to pass the time of day alone.[2]

Alcohol consumption was generally considered a problem only when it resulted in drunkenness. Since the Native Americans encountered by the Europeans were not used to these intoxicating beverages, they did in fact have a tendency to become drunk on them. Some crafty settlers took advantage of this. They gave the Native Americans large quantities of alcohol and then took their land when they were in no condition to stop the settlers. In an effort to prevent this, laws forbidding the sale of alcohol to Native Americans were among the first prohibition laws in the colonies. As with most of the prohibition laws that would follow, these were difficult to enforce and frequently ignored.

There were laws to deal with drunkenness among the colonists. These were aimed primarily at the person doing the excessive drinking, rather than at the person selling the liquor. Persons guilty of drunkenness might be punished with a lecture from a minister, a fine, an afternoon in the stocks, or even a whipping.

But alcohol was generally considered both good for people and good for the economy. Brewing (the process of making beer) and distilling (the process of making hard liquor) were among the first and most profitable businesses in America. Local governing bodies were able to raise revenue by taxing these industries. One of the other industries the liquor trade became associated with was, unfortunately, the slave trade. Molasses was imported from the West Indies and distilled in New England into rum. Rum and the profits from rum were used to buy slaves in Africa. Many of them were sent to work in the West Indies. This completed what was known as the triangle trade.

One colony that tried to set itself apart from the drinking ways of the others was Georgia. James Oglethorpe led the first group of settlers there from England. He did this with the intent of creating a community that would practice temperance— drinking only beer instead of the hard liquors preferred elsewhere, and only in moderate amounts. But soon the colonists began smuggling in rum from South Carolina and making their own as well. They ignored repeated pleas for restraint from Oglethorpe and even from the British Parliament and king. With so many of the settlers ignoring the law, the governing body of the colony was forced to admit defeat. It began licensing taverns and permitting the legal importation of rum.

Taverns were important meeting places for the colonists. Many of the meetings in which colonists discussed their anger with their British rulers, before and during the Revolutionary War, were held in taverns.

Whiskey or Bread?

When the Revolutionary War cut off shipments of the molasses (from the West Indies) needed to make rum, colonial distillers switched to using rye and corn to make whiskey. Soon there were a lot of people drinking whiskey and drinking a lot of it. Some people feared there would not be enough grain left to make bread. Others feared for the social costs of an increased number of drunkards.

On February 27, 1777, the Continental Congress resolved:

> That it be recommended to the several legislatures of the United States to pass laws putting an immediate stop to the pernicious practice of distilling grain, by which the most extensive evils are likely to be derived, if not quickly prevented.[3]

Dr. Benjamin Rush was a prominent physician who had served in the American Revolution. He took a stand against the popular notion that unlimited alcohol use was good for all manner of illnesses and necessary for good health. He tried to educate people about the medical, moral, and social costs of heavy drinking. In 1784, he published a pamphlet entitled *Inquiry into the Effects of Spiritous Liquors on the Human Body and Mind.* For the next several decades, copies of the pamphlet sold out almost as quickly as they could be printed. He argued that moderate amounts of wine and beer would do little harm. Drinking whiskey and rum, however, would lead to disease and death. He dreamed of a happy, healthy America where these hard liquors were shunned.

After the Revolution, the new American government found a use for

Benjamin Rush was a colonial physician who was among the first to question the popular idea that unlimited alcohol use was actually good for the body and could cure illnesses.

liquor—the raising of revenue. First Congress taxed the importation of molasses and rum. Then it taxed the locally produced whiskey. This upset many farmers, who were experiencing tough economic times after the war. Many farmers found it cheaper to turn their corn into whiskey and sell it that way than to transport the corn over rough wilderness roads to market. They also suspected that the government was trying to keep them from drinking hard liquor. They objected to that interference in their lives. "If any man supposes that a mere law can turn the taste of a people from ardent spirits," said Congressman Fisher Ames of Massachusetts, "he has a romantic notion of legislative power."[4]

This led in 1794 to what became known as the Whiskey Rebellion. Riots broke out in western Pennsylvania as "rebels" terrorized local tax collectors. President Washington rode with some fifteen thousand soldiers to the Pennsylvania countryside and the rebellion collapsed. Both sides had made their point, however. The government proved its right to enforce laws. The people made clear their distaste for this particular law.

Temperance Clubs

In the early 1800s, temperance clubs began to form. Individuals and small groups of people began to profess that they would consume no more distilled spirits. Though technically the word "temperance" means the moderate use of alcohol, the temperance movement came to be associated first with an abstinence from distilled liquor, and then with a total abstinence from any form of alcohol. It soon also became associated with the work of churches as many religious people saw alcohol as a primary cause of sin and an obstacle to salvation.

In 1826, a Connecticut preacher named Lyman Beecher published his thoughts on the subject as *Six Sermons on the Nature, Occasions, Signs, Evils and Remedy of Intemperance*. Beecher appealed to the deepest emotions and beliefs of his readers. He urged them to consider personal health and happiness as well as community and national pride. He saw that excessive drinking grew from moderate drinking. Therefore, he believed that total abstinence was the only solution. He was concerned about the evils that surrounded the sale of liquor in general. He moved to Boston and worked there with others, including the Reverend Justin Edwards, to try to unite small temperance groups around the country into a national temperance society. Edwards spoke before both houses of Congress and even held a temperance rally in the House of Representatives. It was hoped that the example set by national leaders, including John Quincy Adams and Daniel Webster, would increase temperance among the general population.

Throughout this period, there were almost as many ideas about what to do about liquor as there were temperance societies. In some societies, members were allowed to take pledges that allowed them to drink light wines and beer. Others took the pledge of total abstinence from all forms of intoxicating drink. These had the letter "T" for "total" put after their names. They were called "teetotalers," a term that came to mean anyone who drank no alcohol at all.

In the 1840s, a new group formed when several friends who were heavy drinkers set about reforming themselves and other drunks. They called themselves "Washingtonians" after George Washington. At their meetings, drinkers would tell stories of their turn away from drunkenness. Then they signed a pledge to give up all alcohol. Their meetings attracted large numbers of people and a lot of attention. This gave many individuals who had formerly been looked down upon for their excessive drinking the opportunity to be looked up to and praised.

The movement caught hold in many small cities and towns and hundreds of Washingtonian societies were formed. Their meetings and huge mass demonstrations created front-page news around the country. But much of the enthusiasm in scattered towns and rural communities tended to die out as soon as the meetings were over, and within a short time, the Washingtonian movement died out.

The Movement Moves On

The temperance movement itself was ready to move on to the next level. It had begun with appeals to individual drinkers to limit their alcohol consumption. It grew to attempt to have drinkers persuade others to give up drinking. Temperance leaders were now about to turn to politicians and law and to attack the liquor trade itself. If reformers were unable to persuade drinkers to give up alcohol for religious, health, or other such reasons, they would have to go right to the source of the temptation. They would get get rid of the alcohol itself.

Local laws were tried in a number of places. When these proved unenforceable, reformers moved to the state level. The Chief Justice of the United States Supreme Court, Roger Taney, supported state liquor laws. He wrote,

> If any state deems the retail and internal traffic in ardent spirits injurious to its citizens, I see nothing in

> the Constitution of the United States to prevent it from regulating and restraining the traffic, or from prohibiting it altogether, if it thinks proper.[5]

In 1851, a law was passed forbidding the manufacture and sale of any intoxicating liquor in the state of Maine. In the next four years, twelve states adopted similar laws. But in many cases, the victories were short-lived. In some states, the laws were ruled unconstitutional. In other states, voters changed their minds and repealed the laws. In many cases, even though there were laws prohibiting liquor, those that wanted it still found ways and places to get it. Still, in many states, some sort of liquor laws would remain on the books.

During the 1850s, the reform that most occupied the minds and discussions of Americans concerned the issue of slavery. Attention turned from prohibition to abolition—an end to slavery. During the Civil War, the government once again found a use for alcohol. On July 1, 1862, President Lincoln signed the Internal Revenue Act. It charged a fee on all retail liquor establishments (more commonly known as taverns or saloons) and a tax by the gallon on the manufacture of liquor and beer. This was done to raise money for the war.

Opponents pointed out that it amounted to government approval of the liquor trade. Senator Pomeroy of Kansas said that with the granting of a license:

> The man who pays his twenty dollars can go about the community with perfect impunity and can make as many widows and orphans and produce as much poverty, degradation and crime as he chooses. He has paid twenty dollars for the privilege of doing it.[6]

Temperance leaders were especially distressed since Lincoln had previously been considered a champion of temperance.

During the Civil War, President Lincoln tried to raise money through the passage of the Internal Revenue Act. Among other things, the act imposed a fee on all places that served liquor, such as the saloon shown here.

Like many temporary measures, it ended up hanging around long after the emergency that sparked it was over. For the next fifty some years, until the early 1900s, it would remain an important source of funds for the federal government. It also gave the liquor traffic, which the temperance movement had worked so hard to discredit, a new sort of respectability.

Time for a Political Party

After the war, a number of temperance leaders decided the time had come to form a political party dedicated to the fight against alcohol. The National Prohibition Party was formed in 1869. Its primary purpose was to work for prohibition. It was also in favor of the vote for women and the direct election of senators. These reforms would all eventually find their way into constitutional amendments.

In 1872, the first National Prohibition Party candidate for the presidency was James Black, a lawyer from Pennsylvania. Neither Black nor future candidates would receive large numbers of votes. The Prohibition Party, however, did contribute to acceptance of the idea that the Constitution should be amended to outlaw alcohol.

The two major political parties refused at this time to take a stand for prohibition. The Republican candidate was the hard-drinking Ulysses S. Grant, running for a second term. The Democrats nominated the eccentric New York newspaperman Horace Greeley. Grant won reelection easily, and the federal government remained uninvolved with prohibition.

The Women's Crusade

In 1873, women in a number of towns in New York, Pennsylvania, and Ohio heard a doctor named Dio Lewis speak. He talked about his belief that women could close the saloons of America if they took to the streets to do it. On December 23, 1873, he spoke in a quiet little town called Hillsboro, Ohio. More than sixty women stood up at the end of his lecture to answer his call to close the saloons. The next day, they chose Mrs. Eliza Thompson, the town's most prominent woman, to lead them. After reading from the Bible and saying a prayer, she led the women of Hillsboro out of the church they had gathered in, singing a hymn.

With song, prayer, and tears, the women marched down the main street of town to the drugstores where liquor was sold. Then they went to the saloons. Mrs. Thompson would report that "by continuous daily

As this political cartoon shows, women were thought of as the strongest advocates of temperance and the fiercest enemies of alcohol.

visitations with persuasion, prayer, song and Scripture-reading, the drinking places of the town were reduced from thirteen to one drugstore, one hotel, and two saloons, and they sold very cautiously."[7]

In town after town, women like them took to the streets. They marched from saloon to saloon, until the movement had become known as the Women's Crusade. Usually, the women stood or knelt in front of a saloon, singing hymns and praying. Sometimes they actually went inside the establishment. This was an action unheard of for refined women of that time.

Often, the women met with a great deal of resistance. This included name calling; obscene jokes and remarks; pushing; pulling of hair; ripping of clothes; being pelted with rotten eggs or soaked with water, beer, or worse; and even being jailed. Still, the women came back—and in ever greater numbers than before.

Between January and July 1874, thousands of saloons, perhaps as many as twenty or thirty thousand, were closed, thanks to the Women's Crusade. But as with earlier temperance victories, permanent success remained elusive. Within a year, many of the saloons had either reopened or been replaced with new establishments. Nothing had really changed. Or had it?

Generally, there seemed an increasing acceptance of the notion that saloons, with all their evils, had to go. And more importantly perhaps, large numbers of women had found a voice in the movement.

One of those women, Miss Frances E. Willard, would call the Women's Crusade the "whirlwind of the Lord." She said that "It has set forces in motion which each day become more potent, and will sweep on until the rum power in America is overthrown."[8] We turn now to her story.

Leaders in the Fight

This chapter takes a closer look at the lives of some of the temperance leaders whose work led to the enactment of the Eighteenth Amendment.

Frances Willard

One of the most important temperance leaders was Frances Elizabeth Willard. She was born on September 23, 1839, in a small town in New York. By the time she was seven years old, the family had moved west, first to Oberlin, Ohio, and then to a farm near Janesville, Wisconsin. It was there, at a place called Forest Home, that Frances grew up playing with her brother, Oliver, and sister, Mary. It was a happy childhood in which work and play and learning were often going on together. Eventually, there was "real" schooling, first with a tutor at home and then in a little schoolhouse Mr. Willard had built a mile from their home. After attending Milwaukee Female College and Northwestern Illinois Female College, Frances later taught at the little schoolhouse that her father had built. She taught at a number of other places also, before eventually becoming dean of women at Northwestern University in Evanston, Illinois.

In 1874, she left Northwestern and soon turned to the cause of temperance. She would fight for this cause for the rest of her life. It was a cause she had first become aware of as a small child. She saw the pledge certificate that hung on the dining room wall. It verified that her father, Josiah Willard, was a member of the Washingtonian Society. He was a total abstainer from alcohol.

Her interest was aroused again when she began hearing stories of the Women's Crusade in Ohio. She traveled to Boston to speak with Dr. Dio Lewis. He was the man who had sparked the Women's Crusade with his challenge that women could close saloons if they made up their minds to do so. From there, she went to Pittsburgh. While visiting friends there, she joined a group of Crusaders as they invaded a saloon. In her autobiography, she wrote:

> At a signal from our gray-haired leader, a sweet-voiced woman began to sing 'Jesus the Water of Life will Give,' all our voices soon blending in that sweet song. . . . [Then] a sorrowful old lady whose only son had gone to ruin through that very death-trap, knelt on the cold, moist pavement and offered a broken-hearted prayer.[1]

When Frances Willard returned to Illinois, she became president of the Chicago branch of the Women's Christian Temperance Union (WCTU). She turned down a number of respectable and financially rewarding teaching positions to become, as she put it, "leader of a forlorn hope."[2]

In the fall of 1874, women from seventeen states gathered in Cleveland. They were there to organize the national Women's Christian Temperance Union.

Inspired by her father, who totally abstained from alcohol, Frances Willard became one of the most famous opponents of saloons in the early days of the temperance movement.

Frances Willard became the first corresponding secretary. In 1879, she was elected national president of the WCTU. Under her leadership, it became one of the most powerful temperance organizations in the United States. As she branched out internationally, it also became powerful in other countries. Willard encouraged women of all classes, ages, and interests to join. Besides working for temperance, the WCTU promoted physical exercise for women and other improvements in family health and welfare. In fact, everything Frances Willard did was focused on protecting the home and family.

She once said, "We have the tariff to protect industry, patent laws for the inventor, land grants for railways, but for the homes of America we have no adequate protection from the [saloons]."[3] She was asked to speak all over the country. She was known for a seemingly inexhaustible supply of energy. She became one of the best-known people of her time. She became president of the world WCTU in 1891. She was asked to speak on behalf of her beloved causes in Europe as well.

When Willard turned fifty in 1889, her friends begged her to write her autobiography. For the next few months, she poured her energy into this work. She produced a book of twelve hundred pages (cut by the editors to seven hundred), which she called *Glimpses of Fifty Years.*

Years of passionate work had taken their toll, however. By age fifty-nine, she was exhausted and in poor health. She died on February 17, 1898, at fifty-nine years old. With new leadership, the WCTU became much less radical and more closely focused on prohibition. In 1905, Frances Willard became the first woman to have her statue placed in Statuary Hall in the United States Capitol.

Billy Sunday

Billy Sunday was born in Iowa on November 19, 1862. His father was away serving in the Civil War at the time, and eventually died of illness on December 22, 1862, never having seen his son. Young Billy spent his earliest years on his grandfather's farm. When his mother found it difficult to care for him and his brother, they were sent to an orphanage for soldiers' children for a few years.

As Billy grew up, he loved to play baseball. A neighbor would remember, "Many people here insist that the world has never produced as good a ball-player. His position was center-field. He was a sure batter and a good base-runner. What was a one base hit for others, was a two-bagger for him."[4]

In 1883, he became a member of the Chicago White Sox. He played there for five years before moving on to Pittsburgh and then Philadelphia. He was generally considered a nice guy. He was well liked by his colleagues, but not especially religious.

In his own words, Billy Sunday would tell how his life changed on a fateful night in Chicago in 1887. He would recall the following:

> I walked down a street in Chicago with some ball players and we went into a saloon. It was a Sunday afternoon and we got tanked up, and then went and sat down on a corner. Across the street a company of men and women were playing on instruments, and others were singing the gospel hymns that I used to hear my mother sing in Iowa, and back in the old church where I used to go to Sunday school. And God painted on the canvas of my memory a vivid picture of the scenes of other days and other faces. I sobbed and sobbed and a

Billy Sunday (left), a former baseball player who had spent a great deal of his career drinking, became a sermonizer in the fight against alcohol following his retirement from the sport. Sunday's sermons, and the energetic way he presented them, brought the prohibition movement many new supporters.

young man stepped out and said: "We are going down to the Pacific Garden Mission; won't you come down to the mission?

I arose and said to the boys: "I'm through. We've come to the parting of the ways," and I turned my back on them.[5]

From that time on, he would combine working for God with fighting the alcohol that had nearly ruined him. One of the first changes for the reformed Billy Sunday was that he refused to play baseball on Sunday. This was something he was able to get away with because he was a good player. In 1891, though, he decided to leave baseball altogether. He took a huge cut in pay to go to work for a religious organization in Chicago. He began to give sermons in churches and at religious revivals. People loved the way he talked in everyday language. They also loved the way he jumped and shouted and waved his hands when he spoke. Though he had quit baseball, he continued to use his athletic gifts.

He developed a number of standard sermons, which he would deliver over and over again. One of the more famous became known as his "booze sermon." His biographer reported:

Probably no single sermon in any preacher's career has been so frequently repeated, so widely read and circulated, and so generally made the subject of comment. Upon occasions Mr. Sunday has preached this sermon, which requires about an hour and a half for its delivery, three times in the same day. As many as 50,000 people have heard it between daylight and dark. It is the sermon most frequently demanded of him when he goes out to do campaigning in any state. In pamphlet form it has been sold by the tens of thousands for many years.[6]

Just imagine him standing on a stage before a spellbound crowd as he shouted while pounding one fist into the palm of his other hand:

> Seventy-five percent of our idiots come from intemperate parents; . . . eighty-two percent of the crime is committed by men under the influence of liquor; ninety percent of the adult criminals are whisky-made. . . . I go to a family and it is broken up, and I say, "What caused this? Drink! . . . Whence all the misery and sorrow and corruption? Invariably it is drink."

Pointing a finger at an invisible enemy, he would continue:

> The saloon is the sum of all villainies. It is worse than war or pestilence. It is the parent of crimes and the mother of sins. And to license such an incarnate fiend of hell is the dirtiest, low-down damnable business on top of this old earth.[7]

For some forty years, he went on preaching and was credited with almost a quarter of a million conversions. He preached his last sermon one week before he died on November 6, 1935, at the age of seventy-two.

Carry Nation

Carry Amelia Moore was born on a Kentucky farm on November 25, 1846. Her father moved the family first to Kansas, then to Texas, and finally to Missouri. Hers was not a particularly pleasant childhood and youth. Difficult economic times forced her to work hard, and her mother was not easy to get along with. Carry also suffered from many mysterious illnesses as she was growing up.

In November 1867, she married a doctor named Charles Gloyd. She had been warned that he was a heavy drinker, but she did not believe it because she

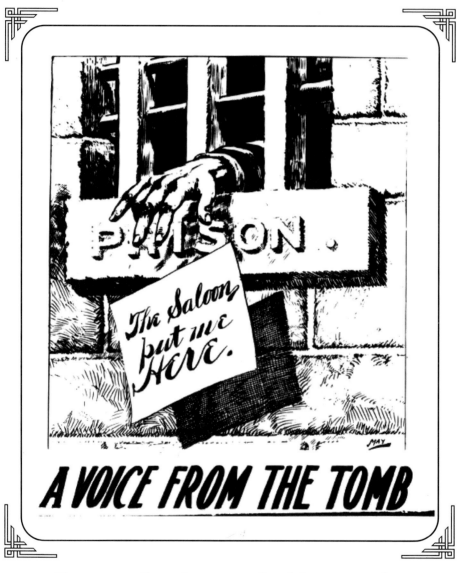

This poster reflects the opinion of prohibitionists such as Billy Sunday, who felt that most of the crime and suffering in the United States could be traced back to alcohol.

had never seen him drunk. On their wedding day however, he arrived drunk and remained that way much of the time thereafter. He seldom worked, there was little money or food, and soon Carry was expecting their child. By the time their daughter was born in September 1868, Carry had left her husband and was living on her parents' farm. Within six months, her husband died a drunkard's death.

About a year later, Carry married David Nation, a lawyer and minister. They were very different people and bickered frequently. Each had thought the other would solve their problems and it just was not to be so. After a number of moves and many hard times, they ended up in Medicine Lodge, Kansas.

In May 1892, she was involved in starting a local chapter of the WCTU in Medicine Lodge. The constitution of Kansas made saloons illegal, yet there were plenty of them. One day in 1899, a woman came to Carry crying because her husband spent all their money in one of the illegal saloons. Carry was ready to fight. She marched down to the saloon and prayed loudly in the street before it. She confronted the saloonkeeper. She warned him that he would die and go to hell unless he closed down. That man did in fact flee, but there were still a number of places in Medicine Lodge selling alcohol. Nation made things so miserable for them that within a year they were forced to close as well.

Carry Nation was not finished, however. When she awoke on the morning of June 5, 1900, she believed the Lord told her, "Go to Kiowa."[8] She drove her buggy to a friend's house in Kiowa that afternoon, and the next morning she entered a saloon armed with rocks wrapped in newspaper—"smashers" she called them.

"Men!" she announced as she entered the saloon, "I have come to save you from a drunkard's fate." The men who were gathered around the bar finished their drinks and left. Then she told the saloonkeeper, "Get out of my way. I don't want to strike you, but I'm going to break this place up." She threw a rock at the big mirror behind the bar and it shattered. She proceeded to smash and break all the bottles she could get hold of. As she was leaving, she picked up some more stones and broke the front window. Then she climbed in her buggy and proceeded to another saloon a block away. After making a mess there, she strode into the street and challenged the crowd that had gathered to watch the commotion, "If I have broken a statute of Kansas, put me in jail. If I'm not a lawbreaker—and I'm not a criminal—your mayor and councilmen are, and you must arrest them."[9]

The mayor, the marshal, and the attorneys debated in the street what to do. If they arrested her, there would be a lot of publicity about the illegal saloons. How could they arrest her for destroying property that was being used in an illegal business?

They decided to let her go, warning her that if she came back she'd go to jail. She, in turn, warned them to close the saloons or she *would* be back.

When she returned to Medicine Lodge, she received both cheers and jeers. Most of the WCTU women found her methods too violent for their tastes. Nation, however, was determined to wreck as many saloons as she could. After all, she believed that alcohol and saloons were the source of all her problems, especially her first husband's death. They had wrecked countless other lives as well.

On December 26, 1900, she took the train to Wichita. There she found police officers in the bars

After leaving her alcoholic first husband, Carry Nation
became a fierce opponent of the saloon industry. Often
using violent methods such as swinging a hatchet, Nation
set out to destroy the illegal saloons that operated in open
defiance of the law.

(discreetly called "sample rooms") along with citizens. She proceeded to destroy one of the largest, most elegant bars. This time the police came and hauled her off to jail.

At the police station, the chief acted surprised to hear that there was a saloon operating in Wichita. If Nation would just take the next train back to Medicine Lodge, he would take care of it, he said. Nation laughed in his face and told him she had no intention of leaving until all the saloons were smashed. She was sent to jail. Of this experience, she wrote, "The sensation of being locked in such a place for the first time is not like any other. . . . I tried to be brave, but the tears were running down my face."[10] Carry Nation was fifty-four years old at the time.

On January 18, 1901, she was released from jail and charges were dropped. She rested just two days and then was back in Wichita. This time, she was armed with the small hatchet that would become her trademark. She and a small group of women sang and prayed and proceeded to smash several saloons. For this, they ended up in jail. Carry Nation moved on throughout Kansas and into other states. Neither jailing nor physical attacks nor ridicule would stop her. Between "smashings," she lectured on temperance. She sold souvenir hatchets to make some money. (She and her husband had divorced.) She also published a newspaper called *The Smasher's Mail.* Saloon owners made fun of Carry Nation, naming awful-tasting drinks after her. "All Nations Welcome But Carry," others joked with signs over their doors.[11]

Carry Nation continued her rampage against the saloons for about ten years. One day, completely worn out, she collapsed on stage while speaking in Eureka Springs, Arkansas. "I—I have done what I could," she murmured.[12] She was taken to a hospital in Kansas, where she died on June 2, 1911, at the age of sixty-four.

While her methods may have been unusual, Carry Nation helped focus attention on the evil heart of alcohol—the saloon. She, Frances Willard, and Billy Sunday devoted themselves to exposing that evil and trying to end it. They each used different tactics, but they all agreed that alcohol, and the saloon along with it, must go.

Closing in on Victory

At the same time that some groups were becoming less and less tolerant of alcohol, immigrants were pouring into the United States. Many came from countries like Germany and Ireland, where the consumption of alcohol, beer in particular, was widely accepted. Also, great numbers of Americans were moving from small towns and rural areas to the cities, where life was different and again, moderate alcohol consumption was widely accepted.

The Devil's Headquarters

In just about all parts of the country in the late 1800s and early 1900s, the saloon was a very common part of American life. According to author Larry Engelmann:

> The saloon was never just a place where alcoholic beverages were dispensed. . . . There were more saloons in America than churches, schools, hospitals, libraries, jails, theaters, or parks. More young men grew up to become saloonkeepers than ministers. Every town had its saloons, legal and illegal, open and concealed. They

lined the main streets of towns and cities like starlings crowded on a clothesline.[1]

Many saloons provided services beyond the provision of alcohol. There were newspapers to read, mail service for travelers and regular patrons, information on jobs, friendly conversation, and almost everywhere, a free lunch. But these "benefits" were far outweighed, at least in the minds of prohibitionists, by the evils also encountered there. They often called saloons "the devil's headquarters on earth." Herbert Asbury wrote:

> As an institution the saloon was a blight and a public stench. It was dingy and dirty, a place of battered furniture, offensive smells, . . . and appalling sanitary facilities. It encouraged drunkenness; . . . It ignored the law. It corrupted the police, the courts, and the politicians. It was a breeding place of crime and violence, and the hangout of criminals and degenerates of every type.[2]

According to Asbury, it was not just liquor but the greed of the brewers that was mainly responsible for this situation. "Before prohibition the big money in the liquor business was in beer, and probably no class in America has ever been more greedy for profits than the old-time brewers."[3]

In 1886, an event occurred that showed the stakes involved in the prohibition movement. Reverend George C. Haddock of Sioux City, Iowa, was so effective in his protests against saloons that plans were made at a local saloonkeepers' meeting to get rid of him. A seven-hundred-dollar reward was offered to anyone who would do the deed. A few evenings later, he was confronted by a group of men. One of them pulled out a pistol and killed Reverend Haddock. The man charged with the killing was a brewer. The first trial was declared a mistrial. A juror revealed that he

Saloons such as these were referred to by prohibitionists as "the devil's headquarters on earth," since so much evil and crime seemed to come out of their doors.

and other jurors were offered bribes from the brewer's representatives. A second trial resulted in the accused man being set free, even though it seemed clear that liquor interests again had heavily influenced the jury.

The Anti-Saloon League

During the final decades of the nineteenth century, the temperance movement gathered steam in its fight against these evils. Joining the WCTU and the Prohibition Party in the effort to wipe out liquor was the Anti-Saloon League. It was established on a national basis in 1896.

During the 1890s, this organization moved to the forefront of the temperance movement. The Anti-Saloon League was very successful in raising funds, largely through church organizations. It appealed to church members in small towns all across the country to make their local, state, and national representatives responsive to the temperance movement.

The Anti-Saloon League very successfully merged the religious and political aspects of the cause. Rather than supporting the Prohibition Party, they supported politicians from any party who voted "dry." They produced numerous pamphlets and newspapers filled with antiliquor information. "No citizen should ever cast a ballot for any man, measure or platform that is opposed to the annihilation of the liquor traffic," said one publication. Another urged voters to "rescue our country from the guilt and dishonor which have been brought upon it by a criminal complicity with the liquor traffic."[4] By the turn of the century, the Anti-Saloon League had a growing control over many state lawmakers. It was also working to increase its power at the national level.

The United States Brewers' Association and the

National Wholesale Liquor Dealers Association were ready to spend money to fight the movement. But everything they did appeared self-serving. The temperance movement, meanwhile, could claim the high moral ground of fighting for God and the family. Brewers admitted in their own trade publication that the saloon "has been getting worse instead of better. It has been dragged into the gutter."[5] But they did very little to improve the situation.

In 1881, Kansas was the first state to make prohibition part of its constitution. It was felt that, while laws were fairly easy to change, constitutional prohibition would be permanent. Several other states followed with constitutional prohibition. Still more continued to work on prohibition laws. By 1918, there were twenty-six states that at least had laws regulating the liquor trade.

In most cases, however, these laws were not aimed at absolutely prohibiting all sales of alcohol. They were largely concerned with abolishing the saloon and supervising the liquor trade. As author Charles Merz points out, in each case the methods and the penalties of prohibition varied according to local customs, local standards, and local taste.[6]

Many of the states with prohibition laws were ones in which the population was largely agricultural and rural. They tended to be people who feared that the immigrants and the industrialized cities were changing the United States in ways they did not like. Gradually, prohibition began to appear to be a rural, Protestant religious movement directed against the cities and the immigrants, many of whom were Catholic.

Prohibitionists scored a victory in 1913 with the passage of the Webb-Kenyon Bill. This bill gave dry states the right to stop liquor shipments at their borders. This was expected to help them enforce their anti-liquor laws. Some people thought that this law might be unconstitutional. The Supreme Court later upheld it, however. This law was supposed to make it easier for states with dry laws to keep liquor out. Real enforcement, however, would continue to be a problem.

The Battle for the Constitutional Amendment

With the victory, the Anti-Saloon League decided to focus now on attaining national prohibition. They wanted to move from local control of liquor issues to national control. At the league's convention in November 1913, a resolution was adopted in favor of national prohibition. The league's attorney, Wayne B. Wheeler, reported: "Then the convention cut loose. With a roar as wild as the raging storm outside it jumped to its feet and yelled approval. The first shot in the battle for the Eighteenth Amendment had been fired."[7] Wheeler himself would become the driving force behind the league's efforts. As such, he would become one of the most politically powerful prohibitionists.

In December 1913, a delegation of Anti-Saloon Leaguers and members of the WCTU marched up the steps of the Capitol in Washington, D.C. There they presented a proposal for an Eighteenth Amendment to the Constitution. The amendment would prohibit alcohol. The proposal was referred to committees in both houses of Congress. While the resolution was studied in committee, the league worked to educate the public. It also worked to get supporters elected to Congress who would vote for the Eighteenth Amendment.

Wayne B. Wheeler, general counsel and legislative
superintendent of the Anti-Saloon League of America, was
one of the most politically powerful prohibitionists.
Wheeler was among those who proposed the Eighteenth
Amendment to the Constitution.

According to Wheeler:

We started off with about 20,000 speakers, mostly volunteers, all over the United States. . . . During the final stages of the battle there were approximately 50,000 trained speakers, volunteers and regulars, directing their fire upon the wets in every village, town, city, county and state.

The Anti-Saloon League's printing plant at Westerville "ran three shifts a day, every hour of the twenty-four, grinding out dry literature," and the league "went into every congressional district where there was a chance to elect a dry and waged as strong a fight as candidates have ever seen."[8]

The liquor industry responded with "wet" propaganda of their own. Mostly it emphasized the economic importance of jobs in the liquor industry. It called the Anti-Saloon League "the most arrogant organization of canting hypocrites . . . the world has ever seen."[9] It antagonized the many women who were working for both suffrage and prohibition. "We oppose always and everywhere the ballot in the hands of woman, for woman's vote is the last hope of Prohibitionism," the brewers said.[10]

There were other Americans who were not particularly in favor of prohibition, but they never got organized enough to stop it. Perhaps they thought that the brewers and distillers were rich enough to fight the battle effectively for themselves. In addition, everyone knew how difficult it was to get an amendment ratified. Even if prohibitionists had a lot of support, many people seemed to think that national constitutional prohibition would never become a reality.

A two-thirds majority would be needed in both houses for the constitutional amendment resolution to pass. On December 22, 1914, Congress began debating the resolution. Speeches took from 10:30 A.M. until eleven P.M. Then, a vote was taken. The result was 197 in favor, 190 against. This was not the two-thirds majority needed to pass, but it was an impressive showing nonetheless. It encouraged the league to work even harder during the 1916 election. It campaigned for even more senators and congressmen who would vote in favor of the resolution.

The Patriotic Choice

On April 6, 1917, the United States declared war on Germany, and entered World War I. Drys worked to shut down the liquor industry with wartime prohibition measures. Congress passed a number of wartime prohibition measures. These included a food control bill intended to conserve grain and other food for the war effort. The Anti-Saloon League used the outbreak of the war to their advantage in every way possible. It declared that prohibition would speed victory. Therefore, it was the only patriotic choice. It pointed out that many brewers were German-Americans. It charged the brewing industry with being pro-German.

In the Senate, wets let it be known that they would not object to a vote now on the proposal for the Eighteenth Amendment—on one condition. They insisted that, once the proposal passed in the Senate and the House, it would have to be ratified in six (later modified to seven) years. The drys agreed to this condition, which greatly pleased the wets. They felt sure that half a dozen years would be insufficient for thirty-six states to ratify it. If they could hold off agreement in just thirteen states, they could defeat the amendment.

The Eighteenth Amendment was voted on in the Senate on August 1, 1917. It passed by a vote of sixty-five to twenty. It was then voted on in the House on December 18, 1917. It also passed there, by a vote of 282 to 128.

The amendment then moved on for ratification by state lawmakers. Around this time, a book appeared that clearly stated the prohibitionist case. *Why Prohibition!*, by author Charles Stelzle, contained the following information:

> Drinking lowered industrial productivity and therefore reduced wages paid to workers; it shortened life and therefore increased the cost of insurance; it took money from other bills and therefore forced storekeepers to raise prices in compensation; and it produced half of the business for police courts, jails, hospitals, alms houses, and insane asylums and therefore increased taxes to support these institutions.[11]

Stelzle held that the burden of these social and economic costs for the whole society outweighed any individual right to use intoxicants and legitimized the restriction of personal liberty.[12]

Only a few weeks after the amendment resolution was sent to the states, on January 8, 1918, Mississippi became the first state to ratify the proposed amendment. It would take just over a year to complete the process. That was a remarkably short time, especially considering that wets had thought that seven years would not be enough. On January 16, 1919, Nebraska was the thirty-sixth state to ratify. This completed the necessary three fourths for ratification. Only Connecticut and Rhode Island never ratified it. The Eighteenth Amendment was proclaimed part of the Constitution, and would go into effect everywhere in the United States one year from that date.

The American Issue *was the official newspaper of the Anti-Saloon League. The issue shown here celebrates the league's greatest triumph—the Eighteenth Amendment to the Constitution.*

The vote among state lawmakers had been overwhelmingly in favor of prohibition. The total vote in the senates of the forty-six states was 1,309 to 240—84 percent for prohibition. The total House vote was 3,775 to 1,025—79 percent for prohibition. When the votes of both houses of the forty-six states were combined, the total on ratification was 5,084 to 1,265. More than 80 percent of the representatives of the people, more than four to one, voted for the Eighteenth Amendment.[13]

Now the issue at hand was to draft enforcement laws. These had to make the amendment meaningful without threatening basic freedoms of American citizens. Wayne Wheeler produced the National Prohibition Act. He gave it to House Judiciary

Committee Chairman Andrew J. Volstead of Minnesota to present to Congress. That is how it became known as the Volstead Act.

One of the most controversial aspects of the Volstead Act was its definition of intoxicating beverages as any liquid containing more than one half of one percent of alcohol. This came as a surprise to some who had supported prohibition, thinking it would be directed mainly at distilled liquors. They thought that beer and wine would still be legal.

The Volstead Act passed in the House and the Senate in October 1919. President Woodrow Wilson vetoed it on October 27. He reasoned that the war emergency and the need to conserve grain were over. Congress immediately overrode the veto. America made preparations for prohibition, which would go into effect at one minute past midnight on January 17, 1920. Drys urged wets to "be good sports" and accept prohibition as the law of the land.

It is interesting that there was very little organized protest against the passage of the Eighteenth Amendment, considering how widely it would be violated. The major newspapers carried few reports about it. During 1917 and 1918, they were focused more on the war in Europe than the battle for prohibition. Many wets seemed to think that when the war was over the issue would go away. By the time the war was over, however, prohibition was the law of the land.

On January 15, 1920, the government announced that even privately owned liquor could be seized when prohibition took effect. This would hold true if the liquor was stored in warehouses, safety-deposit boxes, or just about any place besides a private home. So there was a last-minute scurrying to hire vehicles of all

As this political cartoon suggests, the passage of the
Eighteenth Amendment to the Constitution meant that the
United States government had the power to say what
Americans could and could not drink.

sorts to get hidden stashes moved to private homes as the final hours ticked away.

On the last night, drinkers gathered in some bars for their last legal drink. At a place called the Golden Glades in New York City, a coffin was pushed around the dance floor while drinkers threw their emptied bottles and glasses into it. A New York bartender asked a long-standing customer, Congressman Christopher D. Sullivan, "are they really going to enforce it?" "Yes, I think so," was the reply. "There won't be any more liquor." In later years, they would laugh as they remembered the conversation.[14]

While bugles played taps for alcohol, Wayne Wheeler predicted that enforcement would be only a minor problem after the first year. On January 17, a headline in *The New York Times* reported that "John Barleycorn Died Peacefully at The Toll of 12."[15] But that report, it would turn out, was premature.

At five minutes after midnight, a bartender in New York was arrested for serving a last glass of brandy. There were several more arrests in other cities that night, but, all in all, the first night went pretty well. Officials had expected to have some problems after all. Prohibitionists were confident that these problems could be cleared up quickly. Time would show, however, that they greatly misjudged the lengths to which Americans would go to defeat prohibition.

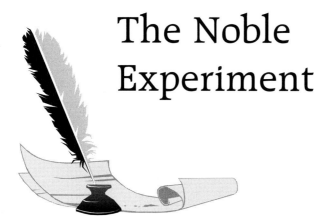

The Noble Experiment

6

It looked at first as if, with a strong show of force, prohibition just might work. After all, most Americans were law-abiding citizens, and many had been living with local and state prohibition laws for some time.

Mr. Elmer Davis of New York remembered,

> Incredible as it may seem, there was a time when Prohibition really prohibited even in New York. For a year or two it was pretty generally observed and observed curiously enough because it did not occur to most people that it was possible to do anything else.[1]

In April 1923, Ida Tarbell reported,

"In the last year I have travelled some thousands of miles in this country, journeys which took me into at least three different states. One sees liquor so rarely that you forget there is such a thing.[2]

But there was indeed such a thing, and those who wanted it found ways to get it. Those who wanted it and those who supplied it would make for an increasingly frightening number of lawbreakers.

A Shot For What Ails You

There were a number of ways to get alcohol. One was by asking a doctor. It was legal for drugstores to sell alcohol to people who had a doctor's prescription for it. Doctors gave out prescriptions by the thousands. In 1928, the Bureau of Prohibition reported that nearly seventy thousand doctors used alcohol prescription books.[3] According to the law, each of the prescriptions for alcohol was supposed to be carefully checked by prohibition agents. There were never enough agents, however, to check even a small percentage of these prescriptions. Thousands of fake prescriptions were also used to purchase alcohol illegally.

The Home Still

Another method was to buy grape juice concentrate. It was sold with directions explaining step by step what not to do to let it turn into wine. For example, one salesperson cautioned: "Do not place the liquid in this jug and put it in the cupboard for twenty-one days, because then it would turn into wine. . . ." From 1925 to 1929, Americans drank more than 678 million gallons of home-fermented wine, three times as much as all the domestic and imported wine they drank during the five years before prohibition.[4]

There were all sorts of other kinds of home brewing and distilling going on as well. "Some economists believed that the sums expended for brewing materials, especially malt syrup, absorbed a large part of the average American household budget."[5]

There were materials available in the library to teach anyone who wanted to learn how to distill alcohol from all sorts of fruits, grains, and even potato peelings. Humorist Will Rogers joked that "the worst crime a child can commit is to eat up the raisins that Dad brought home for fermenting purposes."[6] Many homes contained a one-gallon still. For larger quantities of alcohol, the bathtub could be used.

In the forty years before prohibition, the government seized about fifteen hundred stills a year. Between January and July of 1920, there were 9,553 stills seized—an increase of 1,127 percent.[7] And there were many more stills out there. Government officials admitted that for every still they seized there were at least nine more they never found.

For those who did not have a prescription for medicinal liquor and did not want to make their own, there was plenty of bootleg, or illegal, liquor—you just had to know where to go or who to ask.

"Joe Sent Me"

The old saloons were replaced with supposedly secret drinking places called speakeasies. A speakeasy was simply a place where illegal alcohol was consumed. Speakeasies had existed prior to national prohibition in places where liquor was outlawed by state and local laws. But during the 1920s, the number of speakeasies mushroomed. In some neighborhoods, there were more speakeasies during prohibition than there had been saloons before. As Grover A. Whalen, police commissioner of New York, said, "All you need is two bottles and a room and you have a speakeasy."[8]

"The speakeasy opened the door to a different world, one that shattered old-time barriers in morals and manners," said author Martin Hintz.[9] Young women wore their hair and their dresses short. Young couples danced the Charleston and the lindy and the tango. The 1920s were described as a "decade seemingly gone crazy in the pursuit of fun," and the speakeasy was a big part of the fun.[10] All you had to do was know the secret location and the password to get in. Of course, "Joe sent me" was usually good enough.

All that fun often led to real trouble though. There was always the possibility of getting arrested (and maybe even shot) in a raid. There was also the danger that the illegal liquor being served might make you sick, blind, or even dead. Some speakeasy operators intentionally poisoned their customers. This made them easier prey for thieves who robbed them of whatever they had not spent on overpriced, bad booze. Victims would find it difficult to go to the police. After all, they had been engaging in illegal activities themselves. Inside and outside of speakeasies, individuals who sold illegal liquor were called bootleggers. Until gangsters organized the business, a host of small-time bootleggers competed for trade. "Some estimates put the number of bootleggers nationwide as high as one million. There were too many part-timers, however, to make any figure more than a guess."[11]

Over the Border and Across the Sea

Where did speakeasy operators and bootleggers get their alcohol? Some of it was "good liquor" smuggled in via Canada, Mexico, and all along the Atlantic coast. "Rum runners" brought liquor in boats from the British-controlled Bahama Islands to various places off the Atlantic coast. Bootleggers sailed out from the mainland to meet them. An especially notorious area for this exchange was along the Long Island, New York, and New Jersey shores. On some dark nights, there were as many as one hundred boats waiting for the illegal cargo.

To get an idea of how big a business this was, consider that "before prohibition in the United States, the Bahamas had imported only about fifty thousand quarts of whiskey a year. Within two years its imports had soared to more than ten million quarts."[12] The Coast Guard did what it could to fight this smuggling. It captured thousands of bootlegging boats and their illegal cargoes. It made smuggling more difficult than it would have been otherwise. But the number of bootleggers who worked the coast and the miles and miles of ocean they had to work with made the job pretty much overwhelming.

Federal agents along the land, lake, and river boundaries between the United States and Canada to the north and Mexico to the south also faced a formidable battle. Canada greatly increased the amount of whiskey it manufactured during the 1920s. There was also an increase in the amount of whiskey imported into Mexico. A great deal of this alcohol was then smuggled into the United States.

Near Beer

To add to the supply of smuggled liquor, bootleggers turned to the breweries. It was still legal to brew beer. Virtually all the alcohol was supposed to be taken out, however, before the beer was sold. Some beer was snuck out of breweries before the alcohol was removed. Hypodermic needles were sometimes used to put alcohol back in the "near beer," as beer with most of the alcohol removed was called. It was then called "needle beer." Much of the alcohol that was removed from beer was sold, illegally, and used to create other alcoholic beverages.

Deadly Poison

Then there was industrial alcohol, used in manufacturing. To prevent people from drinking this alcohol, it was denatured. This meant that substances were added to it to make it unfit to drink. Denaturants ranged from the merely obnoxious, such as soap, to the downright deadly, such as sulfuric acid. Many phony manufacturing businesses sprang up. They got permits to receive industrial alcohol legally. They then sold it to bootleggers illegally. The bootleggers tried to convert it, with varying degrees of success, into drinkable alcohol. Many unsuspecting or foolish people were seriously harmed by drinking denatured alcohol. It could cause blindness, paralysis, internal bleeding, and death.

Some people protested that the government should not be putting poisons in industrial alcohol because people who drank it could be harmed. Others felt that people who drank it got what they deserved. As one historian pointed out, "Before prohibition became law, the prohibitionists decried alcohol as a form of deadly poison. After prohibition was law, they approved the legal poisoning of industrial alcohol, knowing full well that men would die from drinking it."[13]

Attempts to Enforce

Warren Harding was elected President of the United States in 1920. As a senator from Ohio, a prohibitionist state, he had voted for the Eighteenth Amendment. While President, however, he was known to have friends over to the White House for card playing accompanied by whiskey. On August 2, 1923, Harding died suddenly. His Vice President, Calvin Coolidge, succeeded him, and was elected on his own in 1924. Coolidge's calm and quiet manner was reassuring to

*With many Americans ignoring the rules of the Eighteenth
Amendment, it was left to agents of the Prohibition Bureau—
seen here with confiscated stills—to enforce the nationwide
ban on the manufacture and consumption of alcohol.*

rural Americans. But he did little better than his predecessor in convincing people that he could enforce the prohibition law.

The Prohibition Bureau was placed under the Bureau of Internal Revenue. Some fifteen hundred federal agents were hired. Their wages were low, their training was minimal, and many were hired because of *who* they knew, not *what* they knew. The bureau started with an annual budget of less than 5 million dollars. It was doubled within five years, but was never nearly enough to combat the problem.

The first prohibition commissioner was John F. Kramer. He was a prohibitionist lawyer from Ohio. He thought that prohibition was the will of the American people. He expected no real problems with enforcement. After a year, he saw things differently. He admitted that prohibition had been "to some extent forced upon large cities in which people had no sympathy whatever with the idea."[14] He soon quit and was replaced by Roy Haynes. Haynes repeatedly issued optimistic statements about the success of prohibition. In January 1922, he announced that enforcement was "rapidly approaching the highest point of its efficiency."[15]

Haynes was a close associate of Wayne Wheeler, who helped keep Haynes in the job. The same could not be said for others in the bureau. Agents around the country quit almost as fast as they could be hired. In one year, it took ten thousand individuals to keep two thousand jobs filled.

Among the most famous federal agents of the Prohibition Era was Eliot Ness. He was head of a special unit known as "The Untouchables." Their famous nickname came from the story that they could not be "touched" or bought off with bribes from gangsters. With careful detective work, Ness and his crew were able to bring Al Capone, the most notorious gangster of the era, to trial.

Another "unit" that earned a lot of publicity was the team of Izzy Einstein and Moe Smith. Working in the New York City area, they made more than four thousand arrests. They also confiscated more than $15 million worth of liquor in four years. Their specialty was disguising themselves as, for example, garbage collectors, opera singers, and college students. In these disguises, they would enter speakeasies and ask for a drink. As soon as they were served, they arrested the bartender.

A few women became prominent among law enforcers. One was Assistant United States Attorney Mabel Willebrant. She had the difficult job of trying to sort through the corruption within the Prohibition Bureau at the same time she was fighting prohibition evaders.

Such able and dedicated enforcement agents were, unfortunately, all too rare. Many agents succumbed to the temptations of bribery. They went to work for the criminals while collecting a paycheck from the government. Others were accused of being overzealous in their use of firearms. Innocent civilians were sometimes killed by mistake in gun battles with gangsters.

Minor prohibition violations clogged the court system. Federal attorneys were spending much of their time on liquor violations. In five years, the unfinished cases on court dockets increased 1,000 percent. Enough arrests were made in a month to occupy all available federal judges for a year. There were estimates that in ten years the courts would be a century behind in their work. Millions of Americans were breaking the law. There was no force on earth big enough to stop them.

The Criminals

Long before prohibition, there had been criminal gangs in many cities, with varying amounts of power.

> Prohibition did not create organized crime. It did, however, create an enormous new area of criminal opportunity that offered less risk and more certain profit than older fields of crime, and produced a general public indifference that lawbreakers had never enjoyed before.[16]

As prohibition went on, the illegal liquor trade was controlled and operated more and more by criminal syndicates, or organizations. One way or another, they eliminated independent bootleggers and speakeasy operators. Those they could not buy out, they terrorized into quitting, or they killed. The tax-free profits in this illegal business were huge. The gangsters would stop at nothing to gain as much money and power as they could.

It was a business that put many of them in the grave. Hundreds of criminals died at the hands of other criminals. So many gangsters were killed at one intersection in Cleveland that it was called Bloody Corner. But it was in Chicago that the words "gangsters" and "prohibition" came to be most closely associated. It was Al Capone who epitomized the greed and ruthlessness of the gangsters.

Alphonse Caponi, better known as Al Capone, was an Italian-born New York tough guy. He came to Chicago in 1919 to work for gangster Johnny Torrio. When Torrio "retired" to Italy in 1925, Capone became the leader of the Torrio gang. He brutally beat to death three rivals on one occasion, and ordered the

Once the manufacture of alcohol was made illegal, it soon became the business of gangsters and criminals to supply the public with the liquor that they wanted. Violence increased as rival organized crime outfits competed for control of the market.

shotgun deaths of many others. He called himself a "businessman," but his business, clearly, was crime and death. He was a chief player in a gangland war that raged in Chicago during the mid-1920s. With the streets of Chicago as a gangland battleground, some five hundred gangsters were gunned down. Capone managed to keep his place at the top of his organization. Gradually, however, he came to symbolize all the criminal evils of prohibition.

Then seven men were gunned down in a garage in Chicago on St. Valentine's Day in 1929. The brutal murders were attributed to Capone's gang. The entire nation was shocked and disgusted. People began to see the gangsters for the cold-blooded murderers they were. They began to demand an end to the activities of these "public enemies." In 1931, Capone was tried and convicted of tax evasion. He was sentenced to federal prison. He was released in 1939, broken in health and spirit. He died in 1947.

A National Disgrace

What had been building into a sort of "national sport"—evading and mocking the Eighteenth Amendment and the Volstead Act—had turned into a national disgrace. Many Americans were fed up with the corruption and violence that prohibition had brought. This was not the "era of clear thinking and clean living" they'd been promised.

7

The Nation
Changes Its Mind

Even before the Eighteenth Amendment was ratified, there were those did not think it was a good idea. Among these was prominent attorney Elihu Root, a former secretary of war and secretary of state. He was among the few leaders to continue to publicly oppose the Eighteenth Amendment even as it was receiving overwhelming support from national and state lawmakers. He claimed that it was unconstitutional. It was an attempt to make laws that should fall under the powers of Congress, not the Constitution. The Supreme Court rejected this argument and upheld the amendment's legality.

Several other challenges to the amendment and the Volstead Act came before the Supreme Court after prohibition went into effect. The Court supported the government's enforcement in each case. It drew attention to some disturbing effects of these acts, however.

In Ohio, a referendum appeared to overturn that state's ratification of the Eighteenth Amendment. The

Congress began to discuss whether prohibition needed to be reevaluated or even overturned. Supporters of the Eighteenth Amendment vowed to keep the capitol "dry," by convincing Congress that prohibition not be ended.

Supreme Court disallowed the referendum results. This controversy gave some people the impression that national prohibition had been forced on the American people against their will.

As prohibition progressed, dry organizations suffered a falling off of interest and of funds. Many prohibitionists felt that their goal had been attained. Their work was now over. With the death of Wayne Wheeler in 1927, the drys lost a powerful spokesman. A clergyman from Virginia, Bishop James Cannon, then rose to prominence in the Anti-Saloon League. He was known for his passionate speeches against the doubters of prohibition. His involvement in several scandals in the late 1920s lessened his influence and became an embarrassment to the league.

The Wets Organize

By that time, the wets were beginning to gather support to fight the lawlessness and corruption spawned by prohibition. The Association Against the Prohibition Amendment (AAPA) grew to be the central group around which the wet opposition gradually formed. Its strength increased year by year. It was founded by Captain William H. Stayton. He believed that "the Constitution is no place for prohibition. That is a local question."[1]

The AAPA was founded in 1918 as World War I came to a close. At first, it was made up mostly of Stayton's friends from his Navy days. Soon he enlisted members of business and social groups in Baltimore and elsewhere. But their efforts were clearly too little too late to stop the ratification of the Eighteenth Amendment. Still, they decided to continue to express their opposition.

It was difficult at this point for anyone to believe

that there was any chance of removing prohibition from the Constitution. No amendment had ever been repealed. All it would take to block a repeal amendment would be one house among the lawmakers of thirteen states. The chances of repeal seemed slim to nonexistent. The Constitution had been written to make amending it difficult. Repealing an amendment was extremely difficult. As late as 1930, Senator Morris Sheppard of Texas, who had helped write the Eighteenth Amendment, claimed, "There is as much a chance of repealing the Eighteenth Amendment as there is for a hummingbird to fly to Mars with the Washington Monument tied to its tail."[2]

As the AAPA considered strategy, they turned to many of the same tactics that had made the Anti-Saloon League so successful in promoting prohibition. The Anti-Saloon League had supported any political candidates who would support prohibition. The AAPA would support any candidates who would oppose it. As their membership grew, this tactic would become more significant.

The AAPA turned to educating people about their stand. In April 1922, Stayton spoke before a large crowd in New York's Carnegie Hall. He called the Eighteenth Amendment "a rotten insult to the American people." It was a law that said that "we can't be trusted." He continued, "This prohibition business is only a symptom of a disease, the desire of fanatics to meddle in the other man's affairs and to regulate the details of your lives and mine."[3] He declared that the Association Against the Prohibition Amendment was actually in favor of temperance and against the evils of the saloon. He felt that Prohibition by constitutional law was resulting in intemperance and even greater evils.

Opposition to the Eighteenth Amendment increased as the years went by. Many people wanted to see an end to the "dry" (alcohol-free) years, and to make the United States "wet" once again.

Since the task of repealing prohibition was so daunting, the AAPA worked in the early 1920s to ease the restrictions of the Volstead Act. In April and May of 1924, hearings on modifying the Volstead Act were held in Congress. Antiprohibitionists urged relaxing Volstead restrictions to allow beer containing 2.75 percent alcohol. Hugh Fox, of the U.S. Brewers' Association, claimed that this would be the "salvation of the prohibition experiment." Legal beer, Fox predicted, would undermine the bootlegging business and bring much greater compliance with the prohibition laws.[4] Prohibitionists called for more effective enforcement of the Volstead Act instead. They refused to compromise at all. The prohibition forces prevailed for the time being.

An Increasingly Ineffective Law

In April 1926, hearings were held before a Senate committee. General Lincoln B. Andrews, the assistant secretary of the treasury, spoke before the committee. He was in charge of supervising prohibition enforcement. His testimony ended up helping the antiprohibition case. He admitted that prohibition agents had engaged in bribe-taking and other forms of corruption. He admitted that many prohibition agents sold and drank alcohol. He also admitted that he agreed with the people who said that modification of the Volstead Act, to allow the sale of light beers, might actually promote temperance. The evidence presented to the committee showed growing rates of violation rather than an increasingly effective law, despite the fact that Congress more than doubled its initial enforcement money.[5]

Nevertheless, the Senate committee decided against any modification of the prohibition laws at this time. The antiprohibition case, meanwhile, continued to grow stronger. In fact, the AAPA began to move away from modification. More and more, it fought directly for outright repeal on the basis that the Eighteenth Amendment was unacceptable.

There had been many different reasons to support prohibition. Different groups focused on different reasons. There were a variety of reasons to fight it, and again different groups focused on different reasons. By the end of the 1920s, the leadership of the AAPA included many of the richest and most powerful people in America. Bank directors, insurance investors, automobile makers were among them. Many of these wealthy citizens were in favor of repeal because they wanted to cut their taxes. The estimated one-half billion dollars a year in liquor revenues not being collected because of prohibition was replaced mainly by their income taxes.

The Crusaders was an organization formed in Ohio in 1929. Its members were outraged by the corruption of prohibition. They hoped to find a solution that would still promote temperance.

Surprisingly, women, who had been such prominent leaders in the temperance movement, were also beginning to join the ranks of the antiprohibitionists. Pauline Sabin was president of the Women's National Republican Club and wife of a wealthy banker. She left her Republican party work and formed the Women's Organization for National Prohibition Reform (WONPR) in 1929.

Sabin, a mother of two boys, explained why she had supported prohibition at first, and then changed her mind. "I was carried away," she said, "by the word pictures of enthusiasts who depicted what the world would be like with no liquor in it." She soon decided, though, that "these pictures were mirages," and that the question of whether her boys were ever to drink liquor should not be the government's responsibility, but her own.[6]

It seemed that everyone had an opinion about prohibition and everyone wanted to talk about it. Ida Tarbell, the journalist who had written that "one sees liquors so rarely" in 1923, now saw things differently. "Is Prohibition Forcing Civil War?" she asked in 1929. "There have been weeks in recent months when the outline of a day's news read like a war communiqué," she claimed.[7]

The growing list of complaints against prohibition included the following: uncontrolled crime, loss of tax revenue, misuse of the Constitution, too much federal authority, and corruption of youth. It also seemed that prohibition had actually reversed the trend toward moderation in drinking of preprohibition days. Prohibitionists claimed that the law simply needed more time and more enforcement to be effective. Both sides circulated as much propaganda as they could. Conflicting claims only added to the confusion and frustration.

The 1928 Campaign

The frustrations with prohibition came to a head politically during the 1928 presidential campaign. The Democratic candidate was New York's Governor Alfred E. Smith. Smith was the product of big-city politics. He was the son of an immigrant, and he was a Catholic. None of this endeared him to rural, Protestant, native-born Americans. He called for modification of the Volstead Act. He made it clear, however, that he would not be opposed to an end to national prohibition altogether.

The only way to end prohibition would be to elect officials who supported a new amendment to overturn it. Supporters of prohibition, such as the Eighteenth Amendment League, took great efforts by encouraging people, especially women (who had gained the right to vote with the Nineteenth Amendment), to vote for those who shared their views.

Smith was opposed in the election by Republican Herbert Hoover. Hoover had managed food distribution to Europe during World War I. He was a self-made millionaire who was expected to help continue the economic prosperity of the 1920s into the 1930s. He also supported continued enforcement of prohibition. He called prohibition "a great social and economic experiment, noble in motive and far-reaching in purpose."[8] He helped link the Republican party with the Eighteenth Amendment. Hoover won in forty of the forty-eight states. Many dry candidates also won election to the Senate and House as well.

President Hoover urged the American people to obey the prohibition laws. ". . . No nation can for long survive the failure of its citizens to respect and obey the laws which they themselves make," he warned.[9] Meanwhile, Congress had passed the Jones Bill, which would enforce prohibition with increased fines and prison terms. This added to the growing notion that the Volstead Act was a "harsh and unreasonable statute." This image was further reinforced by several Supreme Court decisions. The *Carroll* decision permitted police to search a car without a warrant. The *Olmstead* decision dealt with police use of wiretapping. These rulings added to a growing impression that government was unable to cope with lawbreakers by using traditional policing methods. It was assuming new powers in order to accomplish its task.

Economic Disaster

Then in the fall of 1929, the stock market crashed. Over the next several years, businesses failed and unemployment skyrocketed. Thousands of banks

The arrival of the Great Depression gave antiprohibitionists a new reason for legalizing alcohol. They felt that the manufacture of alcohol would create jobs for unemployed workers like these, and increase government revenue, while reducing taxes.

closed down. The life savings of millions of Americans were wiped out. The worst economic disaster in American history was a time that would be known as the Great Depression.

The prohibitionists had used the outbreak of World War I to achieve acceptance of the Eighteenth Amendment. The antiprohibitionists now took advantage of the Depression to overturn it. They argued that repeal of prohibition would increase government revenue, reduce taxes, create jobs, and expand markets for farm goods. Humorist Will Rogers was not being funny when he pointed out, "What does Prohibition amount to if your neighbor's children are not eating? It's food, not drink, that is our problem now."[10] With the government sorely in need of money and Americans desperate for jobs, people began looking critically at the tax-free profits of the gangsters and the money being spent on prohibition enforcement.

The Wickersham Commission

In 1929, President Hoover appointed a commission to study prohibition and its enforcement. The commission was chaired by former Attorney General George W. Wickersham. It became known as the Wickersham Commission. For more than a year, the group listened to testimony given in private.

Meanwhile, early in 1930, the House Judiciary Committee began hearings on possible modification of the Eighteenth Amendment. The AAPA research director, John Gebhart, presented an impressive array of evidence on the evil effects of prohibition. He documented increases of drunkenness and crime since 1920. He also showed the adverse impact of prohibition on the legal and penal systems, and the economic burdens of the law. Prohibition had not stopped drinking, Gebhart concluded; "it only increased costs to consumers and diverted profits into the hands of criminals."[11]

And then in January 1931, the Wickersham Commission gave its report to the President. On January 19, Hoover issued a statement regarding the commission's findings. He made it sound like the commission was in enthusiastic support of prohibition. He declared that "the commission, by a large majority, does not favor the repeal of the Eighteenth Amendment as a method of cure for the inherent abuses of the liquor traffic."[12]

The next day, the commission's actual report was made public. It listed all the faults of prohibition. Individually, most of the commissioners expressed the opinion that prohibition was unenforceable. But then, in the commission's official statement of conclusions and recommendations, as a unit, it opposed prohibition repeal or modification to make beer and wine legal. In other words, what they thought individually basically agreed with the antiprohibitionists. Their official conclusion, however, supported the President's position.

This contradiction between the actual findings and the conclusion caused an uproar. It added to the general confusion surrounding the issue of prohibition. The commission was mocked in a piece that appeared in the New York *World:*

> *Prohibition is an awful flop.*
> *We like it.*
> *It can't stop what it's meant to stop.*
> *We like it.*
> *It's left a trail of graft and slime,*
> *It don't prohibit worth a dime,*
> *It's filled our land with vice and crime,*
> *Nevertheless we're for it.*[13]

These unemployed men are lined up waiting for free food during the Depression. With so many Americans out of work and going hungry, frustrations with the failed policies of prohibition increased.

The Eighteenth Amendment Is Doomed

Wets were more convinced than ever that prohibition was a failure that had to be ended. Many drys believed that prohibition had been sabotaged by poor enforcement and should be given more time.

In March 1932, there was a roll-call vote in the House on the question of repeal. The motion failed by a vote of 227 to 187. It demonstrated, however, that support of repeal was significant and growing. With an election coming up, this encouraged the antiprohibitionists to get out the vote for wets.

More and more former prohibitionists were joining the cause. Charles Stelzle, who had written the book *Why Prohibition!* in favor of the Eighteenth Amendment, now conceded, "Like many others who had sincerely believed in what we advocated at that time, I am personally greatly disappointed in the results obtained through its enactment."[14] John D. Rockefeller's family had supported the Anti-Saloon League with over three hundred thousand dollars in contributions. He announced in 1932 that he now supported repeal.

Both major political parties faced the issue at their national conventions in the summer of 1932. The economy and the Depression were the primary issues, but prohibition was important as well. In the Republican party, the debate was between those who wanted the Eighteenth Amendment revised and those who wanted it repealed. Hoover was renominated, and he refused to consider repeal.

A week and a half later, the Democrats dramatically called for an end to prohibition at their convention. In accepting that party's nomination, Franklin Roosevelt said, "This convention wants repeal. Your candidate wants repeal. And I am confident that the United States wants repeal. From this date on, the Eighteenth Amendment is doomed!"[15]

On November 8, Roosevelt won a stunning victory. This was widely perceived as being a mandate for repeal. The "lame duck" Congress wasted no time in testing the water. On December 5, 1932, a resolution proposing to repeal the Eighteenth Amendment with a new amendment was introduced in the House. It received 272 yes votes to 144 no votes. It was only six votes short of the two-thirds majority required to pass. Many of those 144 no voters, however, would soon be replaced with recently elected wets.

Now that they were so close, wets did not want to wait for the new Congress to convene in December 1933. If a resolution to amend the Constitution could get to the states within the next few months, most state lawmakers would still be in session. They could deal with ratification more quickly.

In February 1933, the Senate began debate on the Twenty-First Amendment. Senator Morris Sheppard of Texas, the loyal supporter of prohibition who had predicted it would never be overturned, attempted a filibuster. This meant that he spoke for over eight hours about anything he could think of to keep the resolution to repeal from the floor. At 10:00 P.M., seeing that he stood alone, he quit. Two days of debate followed on how repeal should be accomplished.

The Senate decided on the Democratic Party's plan to have each state call a convention for the purpose of voting on the proposed amendment. It was believed that this would give the most accurate assessment of the will of the American people. This procedure was mentioned in the Constitution, but had never been used. There was much debate over whether Congress had the power to specify, for the first time in history, that the states must use the convention method of deciding on the amendment.

On February 16, the Senate voted in favor of the resolution to send the Twenty-First Amendment to the states by a vote of 63 to 23. Four days later, the House concurred 289 to 121. The proposed amendment was sent to the states to be ratified by conventions whose members were elected specifically to vote on this measure. Because this procedure had never been used, there was a great deal of confusion in the states. The antiprohibitionist group, Voluntary Committee of Lawyers, stepped in with a solution. It created a model bill for state lawmakers to follow for creating ratifying conventions.

Meanwhile, President Roosevelt took office on March 4, 1933. He immediately cut funding for the Prohibition Bureau. He sent a "special message" to Congress, calling for the legalization of beer. This bill modified the Volstead Act. It passed in both Houses and was signed into law by Roosevelt on April 7. The breweries that had stayed in business happily stopped removing the alcohol from beer. They immediately started shipping out "the real thing." Author Martin Hintz describes the scene in Milwaukee, Wisconsin, known as the "Beer Capital of America." "At 12:01 A.M. on April 7, every factory whistle in town blasted away, church bells pealed, and crowds roared. Twenty-three minutes later, despite a snowstorm, a plane took off for Washington with a load of beer for President Roosevelt."[16]

Attention turned to the state conventions. Votes against repeal in thirteen states would be enough to defeat the Twenty-First Amendment. On April 10,

1933, Michigan voted for it. Nine states that had been expected to vote for repeal had done so by early June, but the drys hoped to make their first real showing of strength in Indiana. But Indiana voted two to one to ratify the Twenty-First Amendment, giving repeal its tenth straight victory. Alabama, Arkansas, Tennessee, and Oregon, formerly considered dry states, also joined the wet parade. Senator Sheppard's home state of Texas voted for repeal. Maine, which had had prohibition laws since 1846, also voted for repeal. In just under eight months, thirty-six states had concurred. Utah was the thirty-sixth on December 5, 1933.

Some of the conventions merely met, chose officials, ratified the proposed amendment, and adjourned. New Hampshire completed its work in a breathtaking seventeen minutes. Some states took a little longer as they explained the reasons for repeal. Most frequently they defined the need for repeal in terms long used by the AAPA. The need to restore local self-government, to protect individual rights, and to put an end to crime, intemperance, and social decay were all mentioned. Around the country, there were praises for the convention system of ratification. It appeared to give a true reflection of the will of the people.

In announcing that prohibition was repealed, President Roosevelt said:

> I ask the wholehearted co-operation of all our citizens to the end that this return of individual freedom shall not be accompanied by the repugnant conditions that obtained prior to the adoption of the Eighteenth Amendment, and those that have existed since its adoption.[17]

At a dinner in New York City that night, the directors of the AAPA toasted Captain Stayton and enjoyed their first legal drinks in fourteen years. The next day, the organization was officially dissolved. The rest of the major antiprohibitionist organizations soon did the same. National prohibition was over.

After Repeal

With repeal out of the way, the Roosevelt administration could focus on turning around the economy. Things did not improve dramatically overnight just because of repeal as wets had led people to believe they would. It would take almost a decade and the defense buildup that accompanied America's entry into World War II for the economy to recover.

A few states did choose to remain dry after repeal, for a while anyway. The rest established statewide laws to regulate the sale of alcohol. There are still state and local laws regulating where, when, and to whom liquor can be sold. For example, it is illegal in many places to sell liquor near a school. Many towns have laws against selling alcohol on Sunday mornings. In the 1970s, many states lowered the drinking age from twenty-one to nineteen. This trend was reversed in the 1980s, largely as a result of concern about young people drinking and driving. All states now have twenty-one as their drinking age.

There are still organizations that support

prohibition today. Their efforts are coordinated by the National Temperance and Prohibition Council. The Prohibition Party, headquartered in Denver, Colorado, continues to put forward candidates for political office. The Anti-Saloon League was renamed the American Council of Alcohol Problems. It is financially dependent on churches and their members. The WCTU claims some two hundred fifty thousand members and still holds annual conventions. Some of its business in recent decades had been supporting a Senate bill to require health warnings on liquor bottles, and to prohibit television liquor ads during hours when children are apt to see them. They also opposed a bill that would allow candy makers to put liquor in candy.

A Legacy of Crime

Repeal did not end the problem of crime. One of the things that prohibition left behind was a powerful and wealthy criminal underworld. With liquor taken out of their control, these people expanded into other "businesses," particularly the sale of illegal drugs.

The Number One Drug Problem

Many people would agree with Dr. Charles Schuster, director of the National Institute on Drug Abuse. He said that "alcohol remains the number-one drug problem in the United States."[1] According to the National Council on Alcoholism, alcohol is a contributing factor in more than fifteen thousand deaths and 6 million injuries due to accidents each year. It is also a leading cause of crime. One survey estimates that more than 40 percent of all arrests made by the police are directly related to alcohol. Another study shows that as many as 50 percent of

Prohibition and repeal both failed to eliminate the problems caused by alcohol in America. Alcohol remains the most commonly abused drug in the United States to this day.

prison inmates arrested for crimes such as murder and assault had been drinking when they committed violent acts. The National Council on Alcoholism notes that 63 percent of women who are violently abused by their husbands report that their husbands were drinking when they were violent. Drunk-driving crashes injure more than six hundred fifty thousand people each year, and kill nearly twenty-four thousand others. Of those killed, some thirty-six hundred are teenagers.[2]

Teenage Drinking

Studies have shown that the earlier a child starts drinking, the more liable he or she is to become an alcoholic later in life.[3] Teenage drinkers may grow into adults who hurt others as well as themselves. This is especially true if the drinker decides to get behind the wheel of a car. Studies have shown that alcohol slows hand and foot reaction speed. It also causes a driver to underestimate speed and distance.

A number of organizations have tried to do something about teenage drinking. One such group is called Students Against Drunk Driving (SADD). SADD was founded in 1981. A high school teacher was deeply saddened when two of his students died in car accidents after attending parties where people were drinking. "We are going to stop this cycle of drinking and driving and dying," he told other students.[4] Together, the teacher and students created SADD. Their first concern is to keep young people alive by preventing them from drinking and driving.

Fetal Alcohol Syndrome

Another alcohol-related problem is known as Fetal Alcohol Syndrome. This refers to the damage done to an unborn child, or fetus, when a women who is pregnant consumes alcohol. Babies born to mothers who drink during pregnancy are often smaller than other babies. Some are born too soon, or are stillborn. Others that look fine at birth may have a hard time drinking from a bottle and may cry a great deal. As they grow up, these children may have many physical, emotional, and learning problems—all as a result of the fact that their mother drank while she was pregnant.

A Right to Drink?

As author Amy Nevitt wrote: "We all pay the price for babies born with Fetal Alcohol Syndrome. The National Institute of Alcohol Abuse and Alcoholism estimated in 1993 that it costs $1.5 million per person to deal with problems related to Fetal Alcohol Syndrome over a lifetime. We pay for sheltered homes, special education programs, and social and health care workers to help these individuals and their families."[5]

Should people have the right to drink as much as they want? Most people would agree that rights no longer apply when drunkenness may cause harm to others. Yet this occurs on our highways every day. Does a bartender have the right to deny service to someone who has had too much to drink? Should tavern owners be held liable for customers' excessive drinking at their establishment? These are just a few of the tricky questions that remain following prohibition and repeal.

Prohibition and Repeal

The results of both prohibition and repeal are generally regarded as a mixture of good and bad. Social workers of the time felt that prohibition generally helped the poor. They claimed that "the health and wealth of the workers of America increased and their drunkeness decreased." But prohibition never came close to fulfilling the promises that its supporters had made.

Repeal did not live up to the promises its supporters had made either. Today we are left with many unanswered questions about alcohol use and abuse, and about whether it is right or wrong to try to make laws to govern morality.

Above all else, however, the story of the Eighteenth and Twenty-First Amendments can be seen as a triumph for democracy. The so-called noble experiment demonstrated that in a democracy, no law can survive without the willing support of the vast majority of citizens.

As author Donald A. Ritchie wrote in his book *The U.S. Constitution,* "Americans take pride in having the world's oldest written Constitution, which has carried our nation through wars, vast territorial expansion, and enormous economic and social change."[6] It has even carried us through a noble experiment, and when that experiment failed, it was able to be changed.

THE CONSTITUTION OF THE UNITED STATES

The text of the Constitution is presented here. All words are given their modern spelling and capitalization. Brackets [ ] indicate parts that have been changed or set aside by amendments.

Preamble

We the people of the United States, in order to form a more perfect Union, establish justice, insure domestic tranquility, provide for the common defense, promote the general welfare, and secure the blessings of liberty to ourselves and our posterity, do ordain and establish this Constitution for the United States of America.

ARTICLE I
The Legislative Branch

Section 1. All legislative powers herein granted shall be vested in a Congress of the United States, which shall consist of a Senate and House of Representatives.

The House of Representatives

Section 2. (1) The House of Representatives shall be composed of members chosen every second year by the people of the several states, and the electors in each state shall have the qualifications requisite for electors of the most numerous branch of the state legislature.

(2) No person shall be a representative who shall not have attained the age of twenty-five years, and been seven years a citizen of the United States, and who shall not, when elected, be an inhabitant of that state in which he shall be chosen.

(3) Representatives and direct taxes shall be apportioned among the several states which may be included within this Union, according to their respective numbers, [which shall be determined by adding to the whole number of free persons, including those bound to service for a term of years, and excluding Indians not taxed, three-fifths of all other persons]. The actual enumeration shall be made within three years after the first meeting of the Congress of the United States, and within every subsequent term of ten years, in such manner as they shall by law direct. The number of representatives shall not exceed one for every thirty thousand, but each state shall have at least one representative; [and until such enumeration shall be made, the state of New Hampshire shall be entitled to choose three, Massachusetts eight, Rhode Island and Providence Plantations one, Connecticut five, New York six, New Jersey four, Pennsylvania eight, Delaware one, Maryland six, Virginia ten, North Carolina five, South Carolina five, and Georgia three].

(4) When vacancies happen in the representation from any state, the executive authority thereof shall issue writs of election to fill such vacancies.

(5) The House of Representatives shall choose their Speaker and other officers; and shall have the sole power of impeachment.

The Senate

Section 3. (1) The Senate of the United States shall be composed of two senators from each state, [chosen by the legislature thereof,] for six years; and each senator shall have one vote.

(2) Immediately after they shall be assembled in consequence of the first election, they shall be divided as equally as may be into three classes. The seats of the senators of the first class shall be vacated at the expiration of the second year, of the second class at the expiration of the fourth year, and of the third class at the expiration of the sixth year, so that one-third may be chosen every second year; [and if vacancies happen by resignation, or otherwise, during the recess of the legislature of any state, the executive thereof may make temporary appointments until the next meeting of the legislature, which shall then fill such vacancies].

(3) No person shall be a senator who shall not have attained to the age of thirty years, and been nine years a citizen of the United States, and who shall not, when elected, be an inhabitant of that state for which he shall be chosen.

(4) The Vice President of the United States shall be president of the Senate, but shall have no vote, unless they be equally divided.

(5) The Senate shall choose their other officers, and also a president *pro tempore*, in the absence of the Vice President, or when he shall exercise the office of President of the United States.

(6) The Senate shall have the sole power to try all impeachments. When sitting for that purpose, they shall be on oath or affirmation. When the President of the United States is tried, the Chief Justice shall preside: and no person shall be convicted without the concurrence of two-thirds of the members present.

(7) Judgement in cases of impeachment shall not extend further than to removal from office, and disqualification to hold and enjoy any office of honor, trust, or profit under the United States: but the party convicted shall nevertheless be liable and subject to indictment, trial, judgement and punishment, according to law.

Organization of Congress

Section 4. (1) The times, places and manner of holding elections for senators and representatives, shall be prescribed in each state by the legislature thereof; but the Congress may at any time by law make or alter such regulations, [except as to the places of choosing senators].

(2) The Congress shall assemble at least once in every year, [and such meeting shall be on the first Monday in December], unless they shall by law appoint a different day.

Section 5. (1) Each house shall be the judge of the elections, returns and qualifications of its own members, and a majority of each shall constitute a quorum to do business; but a smaller number may adjourn from day to day, and may be authorized to compel the attendance of absent members, in such manner, and under such penalties as each house may provide.

(2) Each house may determine the rules of its proceedings, punish its members for disorderly behavior, and, with the concurrence of two-thirds, expel a member.

(3) Each house shall keep a journal of its proceedings, and from time to time publish the same, excepting such parts as may in their judgement require secrecy; and the yeas and nays of the members of either house on any question shall, at the desire of one-fifth of those present, be entered on the journal.

(4) Neither house, during the session of Congress, shall, without the consent of the other, adjourn for more than three days, nor to any other place than that in which the two houses shall be sitting.

Section 6. (1) The senators and representatives shall receive a compensation for their services, to be ascertained by law, and paid out of the treasury of the United States. They shall in all cases, except treason, felony and breach of the peace, be privileged from arrest during their attendance at the session of their respective houses, and in going to and returning from the same; and for any speech or debate in either house, they shall not be questioned in any other place.

(2) No senator or representative shall, during the time for which he was elected, be appointed to any civil office under the authority of the United States, which shall have been created, or the emoluments whereof shall have been increased during such time; and no person holding any office under the United States shall be a member of either house during his continuance in office.

Section 7. (1) All bills for raising revenue shall originate in the House of Representatives; but the Senate may propose or concur with amendments as on other bills.

(2) Every bill which shall have passed the House of Representatives and the Senate, shall, before it become a law, be presented to the President of the United States; if he approve he shall sign it, but if not he shall return it, with his objections to that house in which it shall have originated, who shall enter the objections at large on their journal, and proceed to reconsider it. If after such reconsideration two-thirds of that house shall agree to pass the bill, it shall be sent, together with the objections, to the other house, by which it shall likewise be reconsidered, and if approved by two-thirds of that house, it shall become a law. But in all such cases the votes of both houses shall be determined by yeas and nays, and the names of the persons voting for and against the bill shall be entered on the journal of each house respectively. If any bill shall not be returned by the President within ten days (Sundays excepted) after it shall have been presented to him, the same shall be a law, in like manner as if he had signed it, unless the Congress by their

adjournment prevent its return, in which case it shall not be a law.

(3) Every order, resolution, or vote to which the concurrence of the Senate and House of Representatives may be necessary (except on a question of adjournment) shall be presented to the President of the United States; and before the same shall take effect, shall be approved by him, or being disapproved by him, shall be repassed by two-thirds of the Senate and House of Representatives, according to the rules and limitations prescribed in the case of a bill.

Powers Granted to Congress

The Congress shall have power:

Section 8. (1) To lay and collect taxes, duties, imposts and excises, to pay the debts and provide for the common defense and general welfare of the United States; but all duties, imposts and excises shall be uniform throughout the United States;

(2) To borrow money on the credit of the United States;

(3) To regulate commerce with foreign nations, and among the several states, and with the Indian tribes;

(4) To establish an uniform rule of naturalization, and uniform laws on the subject of bankruptcies throughout the United States;

(5) To coin money, regulate the value thereof, and of foreign coin, and fix the standard of weights and measures;

(6) To provide for the punishment of counterfeiting the securities and current coin of the United States;

(7) To establish post offices and post roads;

(8) To promote the progress of science and useful arts, by securing for limited times to authors and inventors the exclusive right to their respective writings and discoveries;

(9) To constitute tribunals inferior to the Supreme Court;

(10) To define and punish piracies and felonies committed on the high seas, and offenses against the law of nations;

(11) To declare war, grant letters of marque and reprisal, and make rules concerning captures on land and water;

(12) To raise and support armies, but no appropriation of money to that use shall be for a longer term than two years;

(13) To provide and maintain a navy;

(14) To make rules for the government and regulation of the land and naval forces;

(15) To provide for calling forth the militia to execute the laws of the Union, suppress insurrections and repel invasions;

(16) To provide for organizing, arming, and disciplining the militia, and for governing such part of them as may be employed in the service of the United States, reserving to the states respectively, the appointment of the officers, and the authority of training the militia according to the discipline prescribed by Congress;

(17) To exercise exclusive legislation in all cases whatsoever, over such district (not exceeding ten miles square) as may, by cession of particular states, and the acceptance of Congress, become the seat of the government of the United States, and to exercise like authority over all places purchased by the consent of the legislature of the state in which the same shall be, for the erection of forts, magazines, arsenals, dockyards, and other needful buildings;—And

(18) To make all laws which shall be necessary and proper for carrying into execution the foregoing powers, and all other powers vested by this Constitution in the government of the United States, or in any department or officer thereof.

Powers Forbidden to Congress

Section 9. (1) The migration or importation of such persons as any of the states now existing shall think proper to admit, shall not be prohibited by the Congress prior to the year one thousand eight hundred and eight, but a tax or duty may be imposed on such importation, not exceeding ten dollars for each person.

(2) The privilege of the writ of *habeas corpus* shall not be suspended, unless when in cases of rebellion or invasion the public safety may require it.

(3) No bill of attainder or *ex post facto* law shall be passed.

(4) No capitation, [or other direct,] tax shall be laid, unless in proportion to the census or enumeration herein before directed to be taken.

(5) No tax or duty shall be laid on articles exported from any state.

(6) No preference shall be given by any regulation of commerce or revenue to the ports of one state over those of another: nor shall vessels bound to, or from, one state, be obliged to enter, clear, or pay duties in another.

(7) No money shall be drawn from the treasury, but in consequence of appropriations made by law; and a regular statement and account of the receipts and expenditures of all public money shall be published from time to time.

(8) No title of nobility shall be granted by the United States: And no person holding any office or profit or trust under them, shall, without the consent of the Congress, accept of any present, emolument, office, or title, of any kind whatsoever, from any king, prince, or foreign state.

Powers Forbidden to the States

Section 10. (1) No state shall enter into any treaty, alliance, or confederation; grant letters of marque and reprisal; coin money; emit bills of credit; make any thing but gold and silver coin a tender in payment of debts; pass any bill of attainder, *ex post facto* law, or law impairing the obligation of contracts, or grant any title of nobility.

(2) No state shall, without the consent of the Congress, lay any imposts or duties on imports or exports, except what may be absolutely necessary for executing its inspection laws: and the net produce of all duties and imposts, laid by any state on imports or exports, shall be for the use of the treasury of the United States, and all such laws shall be subject to the revision and control of the Congress.

(3) No state shall, without the consent of Congress, lay any duty of tonnage, keep troops, or ships of war in time of peace, enter into any agreement or compact with another state, or with a foreign power, or engage in war, unless actually invaded, or in such imminent danger as will not admit of delay.

Article II
The Executive Branch

Section 1. (1) The executive power shall be vested in a President of the United States of America. He shall hold his office during the term of four years, and, together with the Vice President, chosen for the same term, be elected as follows:

(2) Each state shall appoint, in such manner as the legislature thereof may direct, a number of electors, equal to the whole number of senators and representatives to which the state may be entitled in the Congress: but no senator or representative, or person holding an office of trust or profit under the United States, shall be appointed an elector.

(3) [The electors shall meet in their respective states, and vote by ballot for two persons, of whom one at least shall not be an inhabitant of the same state with themselves. And they shall make a list of all the persons voted for, and of the number of votes for each; which list they shall sign and certify, and transmit sealed to the seat of government of the United States, directed to the president of the Senate. The president of the Senate shall, in the presence of the Senate and House of Representatives, open all the certificates, and the votes shall then be counted. The person having the greatest number of votes shall be the President, if such number be a majority of the whole number of electors appointed; and if there be more than one who have such majority, and have an equal number of votes, then the House of Representatives shall immediately choose by ballot one of them for President; and if no person have a majority, then from the five highest on the list the said House shall in like manner choose the President. But in choosing the President, the votes shall be taken by states, the representation from each state having one vote; a quorum for this purpose shall consist of a member or members from two-thirds of the states, and a majority of all the states shall be necessary to a choice. In every case, after the choice of the President, the person having the greatest number of votes of the electors shall be the Vice President. But if there should remain two or more who have equal votes, the Senate shall choose from them by ballot the Vice President.]

(4) The Congress may determine the time of choosing the electors, and the day on which they shall give their votes; which day shall be the same throughout the United States.

(5) No person except a natural-born citizen, or a citizen of the United States, at the time of the adoption of this Constitution, shall be eligible to the office of President; neither shall any person be eligible to that office who shall not have attained to the age of thirty-five years, and been fourteen years a resident within the United States.

(6) In case of the removal of the President from office, or of his death, resignation, or inability to discharge the powers and duties of the said office, the same shall devolve on the Vice President, and the Congress may by law provide for the case of removal, death, resignation, or inability, both of the President and Vice President, declaring what officer shall then act as President, and such officer shall act accordingly, until the disability be removed, or a President shall be elected.

(7) The President shall, at stated times, receive for his services, a compensation, which shall neither be increased nor diminished during the period for which he shall have been elected, and he shall not receive within that period any other emolument from the United States, or any of them.

(8) Before he enter on the execution of his office, he shall take the following oath or affirmation: "I do solemnly swear (or affirm) that I will faithfully execute the office of the President of the United States, and will to the best of my ability, preserve, protect and defend the Constitution of the United States."

Section 2. (1) The President shall be commander-in-chief of the Army and Navy of the United States, and of the militia of the several states, when called into the actual service of the United States; he may require the opinion, in writing, of the principal officer in each of the executive departments, upon any subject relating to the duties of their respective offices, and he shall have power to grant reprieves and pardons for offenses against the United States, except in cases of impeachment.

(2) He shall have power, by and with the advice and consent of the Senate, to make treaties, provided two-thirds of the senators present concur; and he shall nominate, and by and with the advice and consent of the Senate, shall appoint ambassadors, other public ministers and consuls, judges of the Supreme Court, and all other officers of the United States, whose appointments are not herein otherwise provided for, and which shall be established by law: but the Congress may by law vest the appointment of such inferior officers, as they think proper, in the President alone, in the courts of law, or in the heads of departments.

(3) The President shall have the power to fill up all vacancies that may happen during the recess of the Senate, by granting commissions which shall expire at the end of their next session.

Section 3. He shall from time to time give to the Congress information of the state of the Union, and recommend to their consideration such measures as he shall judge necessary and expedient; he may, on extraordinary occasions, convene both houses, or either of them, and in case of disagreement between them, with respect to the time of adjournment, he may adjourn them to such time as he shall think proper; he shall receive ambassadors and other public ministers; he shall take care that the laws be faithfully executed, and shall commission all the officers of the United States.

Section 4. The President, Vice President and all civil officers of the United States, shall be removed from office on impeachment for, and conviction of, treason, bribery, or other high crimes and misdemeanors.

ARTICLE III
The Judicial Branch

Section 1. The judicial power of the United States, shall be vested in one Supreme Court, and in such inferior courts as the Congress may from time to time ordain and establish. The judges, both of the Supreme and inferior courts, shall hold their offices during good behaviour, and shall, at stated times, receive for their services, a compensation, which shall not be diminished during their continuance in office.

Section 2. (1) The judicial power shall extend to all cases, in law and equity, arising under this Constitution, the laws of the United States, and treaties made, or which shall be made, under their authority; —to all cases affecting ambassadors, other public ministers and consuls;—to all cases of admiralty and maritime jurisdiction;—to controversies to which the United States shall be a party;—to controversies between two or more states, [between a state and citizens of another state;], between citizens of different states;—between citizens of the same state claiming lands under grants of different states, and between a state, or the citizens thereof, and foreign states, [citizens or subjects].

(2) In all cases affecting ambassadors, other public ministers and consuls, and those in which a state shall be party, the Supreme Court shall have original jurisdiction. In all the other cases before mentioned, the Supreme Court shall have appellate jurisdiction, both as to law and fact, with such exceptions, and under such regulations as the Congress shall make.

(3) The trial of all crimes, except in cases of impeachment, shall be by jury; and such trial shall be held in the state where the said crimes shall have been committed; but when not committed within any state, the trial shall be at such place or places as the Congress may by law have directed.

Section 3. (1) Treason against the United States, shall consist only in levying war against them, or in adhering to their enemies, giving them aid and comfort. No person shall be convicted of treason unless on the testimony of two witnesses to the same overt act, or on confession in open court.

(2) The Congress shall have power to declare the punishment of treason, but no attainder of treason shall work corruption of blood, or forfeiture, except during the life of the person attainted.

ARTICLE IV
Relation of the States to Each Other

Section 1. Full faith and credit shall be given in each state to the public acts, records, and judicial proceedings of every other state. And the Congress may by general laws prescribe the manner in which such acts, records and proceedings shall be proved, and the effect thereof.

Section 2. (1) The citizens of each state shall be entitled to all privileges and immunities of citizens in the several states.

(2) A person charged in any state with treason, felony, or other crime, who shall flee justice, and be found in another state, shall on demand of the executive authority of the state from which he fled, be delivered up, to be removed to the state having jurisdiction of the crime.

(3) [No person held to service or labor in one state, under the laws thereof, escaping into another, shall, in consequence of any law or regulation therein, be discharged from such service or labor, but shall be delivered up on claim of the party to whom such service or labor may be due.]

Federal-State Relations

Section 3. (1) New states may be admitted by the Congress into this Union; but no new state shall be formed or erected within the jurisdiction of any other state, nor any state be formed by the junction of two or more states, without the consent of the legislatures of the states concerned as well as of the Congress.

(2) The Congress shall have power to dispose of and make all needful rules and regulations respecting the territory or other property belonging to the United States; and nothing in this Constitution shall be so construed as to prejudice any claims of the United States, or of any particular state.

Section 4. The United States shall guarantee to every state in this Union a republican form of government, and shall protect each of them against invasion; and on application of the legislature, or of the executive (when the legislature cannot be convened), against domestic violence.

ARTICLE V
Amending the Constitution

The Congress, whenever two-thirds of both houses shall deem it necessary, shall propose amendments to this Constitution, or, on the application of the legislatures of two-thirds of the several states, shall call a convention for proposing amendments, which, in either case, shall be valid to all intents and purposes, as part of this Constitution, when ratified by the legislatures of three-fourths of the several states, or by conventions in three-fourths thereof, as the one or the other mode of ratification may be proposed by the Congress; provided [that no amendment which may be made prior to the year one thousand eight hundred and eight, shall in any manner affect the first and fourth clauses in the ninth section of the first article; and] that no state, without its consent, shall be deprived of its equal suffrage in the Senate.

ARTICLE VI
National Debts

(1) All debts contracted and engagements entered into, before the adoption of this Constitution, shall be as

valid against the United States under this Constitution, as under the Confederation.

Supremacy of the National Government

(2) This Constitution, and the laws of the United States which shall be made in pursuance thereof; and all treaties made, or which shall be made, under the authority of the United States shall be the supreme law of the land; and the judges in every state shall be bound thereby, any thing in the constitution or laws of any state to the contrary notwithstanding.

(3) The senators and representatives before mentioned, and the members of the several state legislatures, and all executive and judicial officers, both of the United States and of the several states, shall be bound by oath or affirmation, to support this Constitution; but no religious test shall ever be required as a qualification to any office or public trust under the United States.

ARTICLE VII
Ratifying the Constitution

The ratification of the conventions of nine states, shall be sufficient for the establishment of this Constitution between the states so ratifying the same.

Done in convention by the unanimous consent of the states present the seventeenth day of September in the year of our Lord one thousand seven hundred and eighty-seven and of the independence of the United States of America the twelfth. In witness whereof we have hereunto subscribed our names.

Amendments to the Constitution

The first ten amendments, known as the Bill of Rights, were proposed on September 25, 1789. They were ratified, or accepted, on December 15, 1791. They were adopted because some states refused to approve the Constitution unless a Bill of Rights, protecting individuals from various unjust acts of government, was added.

Amendment 1

Freedom of religion, speech, and the press; rights of assembly and petition

Amendment 2

Right to bear arms

Amendment 3

Housing of soldiers

Amendment 4

Search and arrest warrants

Amendment 5

Rights in criminal cases

Amendment 6

Rights to a fair trial

Amendment 7

Rights in civil cases

Amendment 8

Bails, fines, and punishments

Amendment 9

Rights retained by the people

Amendment 10

Powers retained by the states and the people

Amendment 11

Lawsuits against states

Amendment 12

Election of the President and Vice President

Amendment 13

Abolition of slavery

Amendment 14

Civil rights

Amendment 15
African-American suffrage

Amendment 16
Income taxes

Amendment 17
Direct election of senators

Amendment 18
Prohibition of liquor

Amendment 19
Women's suffrage

Amendment 20
Terms of the President and Congress

Amendment 21
Repeal of prohibition

Amendment 22
Presidential term limits

Amendment 23

Suffrage in the District of Columbia

Amendment 24

Poll taxes

Amendment 25

Presidential disability and succession

Amendment 26

Suffrage for eighteen-year-olds

Amendment 27

Congressional salaries

Chapter Notes

Chapter 1

1. Theodore Thomas Frankenberg, *Billy Sunday: His Tabernacles and Sawdust Trails* (Columbus, Ohio: F. J. Heer Printing Co., 1917), p. 177.

2. Ibid.

3. Paul Sann, *The Lawless Decade* (New York: Crown Publishers, 1957), p. 21.

4. John Kobler, *Ardent Spirits: The Rise and Fall of Prohibition* (New York: G.P. Putnam's Sons, 1973), p. 11.

5. Quoted in Charles Merz, *The Dry Decade* (Garden City, N.Y.: Doubleday, Doran & Co., 1931), p. 51.

6. Ibid., p. 57.

Chapter 2

1. Doris Faber and Harold Faber, *We the People: The Story of the United States Constitution Since 1787* (New York: Charles Scribner's Sons, 1987), p. 50.

2. Donald A. Ritchie, *The U.S. Constitution: Know Your Government* (New York: Chelsea House Publishers, 1989), p. 58.

Chapter 3

1. Quoted in Doris Faber and Harold Faber, *We the People: The Story of the United States Constitution Since 1787* (New York: Charles Scribner's Sons, 1987), p. 135.

2. Paul Sann, *The Lawless Decade* (New York: Crown Publishers, 1957), p. 23.

3. Leigh Colvin, *Prohibition in the United States: A History of the Prohibition Movement* (New York: George H. Doran Co., 1926), p. 13.

4. Quoted in Bill Severn, *The End of the Roaring Twenties: Prohibition and Repeal* (New York: Julian Messner, 1969), p. 23.

5. Ibid., p. 43.

6. Colvin, p. 53.

7. Quoted in Herbert Asbury, *The Great Illusion: An Informal History of Prohibition* (New York: Doubleday & Co., 1950), p. 73.

8. Ibid., p. 86.

Chapter 4

1. Frances E. Willard, *Glimpses of Fifty Years: The Autobiography of an American Woman* (Chicago: H.J. Smith & Co., 1889), p. 340.

2. Ibid.

3. Lydia Jones Trowbridge, *Frances E. Willard of Evanston* (Chicago: Willett, Clarke & Co., 1938), p. 118.

4. Theodore Thomas Frankenberg, *Billy Sunday: His Tabernacles and Sawdust Trails* (Columbus, Ohio: F.J. Heer Printing Co., 1917), p. 30.

5. Ibid., pp. 61, 62.

6. Ibid., p. 175.

7. Billy Sunday, *Billy Sunday Speaks*, ed. Karen Gullen (New York: Chelsea House Publishers, 1970), pp. 53, 54.

8. Quoted in Carleton Beals, *Cyclone Carry: The Story of Carry Nation* (Philadelphia: Chilton Co., 1962), p. 123.

9. Ibid., pp. 127, 128.

10. Ibid., p. 140.

11. Martin Hintz, *Farewell, John Barleycorn: Prohibition in the United States* (Minneapolis: Lerner Publications, 1996), p. 16.

12. Beals, p. 343.

Chapter 5

1. Larry Engelmann, *Intemperance: The Lost War Against Liquor* (New York: The Free Press, 1979), pp. 3–4.

2. Herbert Asbury, *The Great Illusion: An Informal History of Prohibition* (New York: Doubleday & Co., 1950), p. 114.

3. Ibid., pp. 115–116.

4. Martin Hintz, *Farewell, John Barleycorn: Prohibition in the United States* (Minneapolis: Lerner Publications, 1996), p. 21.

5. Asbury, p. 115.

6. Charles Merz, *The Dry Decade* (Garden City, N.Y.: Doubleday, Doran & Co., 1931), p. 23.

7. Quoted in Asbury, p. 115.

8. Quoted in Bill Severn, *The End of the Roaring Twenties: Prohibition and Repeal* (New York: Julian Messner, 1969), p. 89.

9. Hintz, p. 25.

10. Quoted in John Kobler, *Ardent Spirits: The Rise and Fall of Prohibition* (New York: G.P. Putnam's Sons, 1973), p. 204.

11. David E. Kyvig, *Repealing National Prohibition* (Chicago: The University of Chicago Press, 1979), p. 204.

12. Leigh Colvin, *Prohibition in the United States: A History of the Prohibition Movement* (New York: George H. Doran Co., 1926), p. 449.

13. Kobler, p. 16.

14. Kyvig, p. 19.

15. Ibid.

Chapter 6

1. Quoted in Ernest Gordon, *The Wrecking of the Eighteenth Amendment* (Francestown, N.H.: The Alcohol Information Press, 1943), pp. 15–16.

2. Ibid.

3. Andrew Sinclair, *Prohibition: The Era of Excess* (Boston: Little, Brown, 1962), p. 411.

4. Quoted in John Kobler, *Ardent Spirits: The Rise and Fall of Prohibition* (New York: G.P. Putnam's Sons, 1973), pp. 239, 240.

5. Ibid., p. 238.

6. Ibid., p. 241.

7. Sean Dennis Cashman, *Prohibition: The Lie of the Land* (New York: The Free Press, 1981), p. 37.

8. Quoted in Kobler, p. 224.

9. Martin Hintz, *Farewell, John Barleycorn: Prohibition in the United States* (Minneapolis: Lerner Publications, 1996), p. 55.

10. Ibid.

11. Bill Severn, *The End of the Roaring Twenties: Prohibition and Repeal* (New York: Julian Messner, 1969), p 136.

12. Ibid.

13. Richard Hofstadter, introduction to Andrew Sinclair, *Prohibition: The Era of Excess* (Boston: Little, Brown, 1962), pp. vii–viii.

14. Quoted in Charles Merz, *The Dry Decade* (Garden City, N.Y.: Doubleday, Doran & Co., 1931), p. 127.

15. Ibid., p. 123.

16. Severn, p. 140.

Chapter 7

1. Quoted in David E. Kyvig, *Repealing National Prohibition* (Chicago: The University of Chicago Press, 1979), p. 43.

2. Sean Dennis Cashman, *Prohibition: The Lie of the Land* (New York: The Free Press, 1981), p. 229.

3. Quoted in Kyvig, p. 50.

4. Larry Engelmann, *Intemperance: The Lost War Against Liquor* (New York: The Free Press, 1979), p. 189.

5. Kyvig, pp. 61–62.

6. Thomas M. Coffey, *The Long Thirst: Prohibition in America* 1920–1933 (New York: W. W. Norton & Co., 1975), p. 190.

7. Cashman, p. 205.

8. Ibid., p. 192.

9. Quoted in Andrew Sinclair, *Prohibition: The Era of Excess* (Boston: Little, Brown, 1962), p. 363.

10. Martin Hintz, *Farewell, John Barleycorn: Prohibition in the United States* (Minneapolis: Lerner Publications, 1996), p. 76.

11. Kyvig, p. 112.

12. Quoted in Sinclair, p. 365.

13. James P. Barry, *The Noble Experiment, 1919–33* (New York: Franklin Watts, 1972), p. 66.

14. Quoted in Kyvig, p. 152.

15. Quoted in Bill Severn, *The End of the Roaring Twenties: Prohibition and Repeal* (New York: Julian Messner, 1969), p. 172.

16. Hintz, p. 80.

17. Herbert Asbury, *The Great Illusion: An Informal History of Prohibition* (New York: Doubleday & Co., 1950), p. 330.

Chapter 8

1. Jeffrey Shulman, *Drugs and Crime* (Frederick, Md.: Twenty-First Century Books, 1991), p. 67.

2. Ibid., p. 68.

3. Stanley L. Englebardt, *Kids and Alcohol: The Deadliest Drug* (New York: Lothrop, Lee & Shepard, 1975), p. 13.

4. Robert Anastas, *The Contract for Life* (New York: Pocket Books, 1986), p. 25.

5. Andrew Sinclair, *Prohibition: The Era of Excess* (Boston: Little, Brown, 1962), p. 397.

6. Donald A. Ritchie, *The U.S. Constitution: Know Your Government* (New York: Chelsea House Publishers, 1989), p. 15.

Further Reading

Barry, James P. *The Noble Experiment, 1919–33*. New York: Franklin Watts, 1972.

Cohen, Daniel. *Prohibition: America Makes Alcohol Illegal.* Brookfield, Conn.: The Millbrook Press, 1995.

Englebardt, Stanley L. *Kids and Alcohol: The Deadliest Drug.* New York: Lothrop, Lee & Shepard, 1975.

Faber, Doris, and Harold Faber. *We the People: The Story of the United States Constitution Since 1787*. New York: Charles Scribner's Sons, 1987.

Hintz, Martin. *Farewell, John Barleycorn: Prohibition in the United States*. Minneapolis: Lerner Publications, 1996.

Katz, William Loren. *The Constitutional Amendments*. New York: Franklin Watts, 1974.

Landau, Elaine. *Teenage Drinking*. Hillside, N.J.: Enslow Publishers, Inc., 1994.

Monroe, Judy. *Alcohol*. Hillside, N.J.: Enslow Publishers, Inc., 1994.

Nevitt, Amy. *Fetal Alcohol Syndrome*. New York: The Rosen Publishing Group, 1996.

Ritchie, Donald A. *The U.S. Constitution: Know Your Government*. New York: Chelsea House Publishers, 1989.

Severn, Bill. *The End of the Roaring Twenties: Prohibition and Repeal*. New York: Julian Messner, 1969.

Shulman, Jeffrey. *Drugs and Crime*. Frederick, Md.: Twenty-First Century Books, 1991.

Index

Index